GREAT TRAIN
DISASTERS

THE WORLD'S WORST RAILWAY ACCIDENTS

SIENA

GREAT TRAIN DISASTERS

THE WORLD'S WORST RAILWAY ACCIDENTS

Geoffrey Kichenside

This is a Siena book

Siena is an imprint of Parragon

Parragon
13 Whiteladies Road
Clifton
Bristol BS8 1PB

ISBN: 0-75252-630-8

Conceived, designed and produced by Haldane Mason, London

Acknowledgements
Art Director: Ron Samuels
Editor: Charles Dixon-Spain
Designer: Zoë Mellors
Picture Research: Charles Dixon-Spain

Printed in Italy

Picture Acknowledgements
Barnaby's Picture Library © Alexander Apperley: 70; **D. E. Canning:** 11; **Foto-Service SBB**: 38; **The Hulton Getty Picture Library:** 26, 40, 41, 44, 49, 54, 57, 58, 64, 72, 76 (bttm), 77, 92, 93; **Illustrated London News:** 28, 29, 31, 34, 39, 67, 78, 80, 84, 86; **Popperfoto:** 1, 2, 6, 8, 12 (M. Mckeown), 15 (Luc Novovitch), 30, 32, 33 (both), 36, 43, 50, 51, 52, 53, 60, 61, 62, 68, 69, 71, 73, 74, 76 (top) 81, 82, 83, 89, 90, 94, 95; **Mary Evans Picture Library:** 7, 9, 10 (both), 13, 63, 79; *Illustrated London News*: 16, 19, 23, 46; *L'Illustration*: 20; *The Graphic*: 24; *Le Petit Journal*: 37; **Milepost** © Brian Lovell: 14; **Roger Viollet**: 75

Page 1: The Clapham Junction disaster in 1988. 35 passengers died when a train ran into the back of another.

Page 2: The head-on collision at Melun, 28 miles (45 km) south of Paris on 17 October 1991, occurred because the freight train on the right ran past a signal at danger and collided with a passenger train – 16 were killed and 55 were injured.

Contents

CHAPTER 1

WHY DISASTERS SHOULD NOT HAPPEN

Railways offer the safest form of land transport. In many of the years during the second half of the twentieth century not a single passenger has been killed in a train accident in the developed countries. Nowhere is this better demonstrated than in the UK, where no fewer than 12 of the years since the Second World War have seen not one passenger fatality as a result of a train crash. True, in those years passengers have been killed trying to get onto moving trains, others have received fatal injuries falling down stairs on railway property or have killed themselves in their cars when trying to beat trains at level-crossings – ignoring 'stop' signs or weaving around lowered barriers – but these accidents have not been the fault of the railway operators or train crews. In the UK only just over 3000 passengers have been killed in train accidents since the dawn of railways, 150 years ago. Compare that to the UK's annual death toll on its roads in recent years, generally 3500–4000 from all causes, and you realize quite how safe trains are.

Left: Investigators and the media gather at the site of the head-on collision at Silver Spring, Maryland, USA on 17 February 1996, between an Amtrak express and a commuter train, in which 11 people were killed.

Below: The first move towards the steam railway came with Richard Trevithick's pioneering self-propelled steam locomotives first seen at Coalbrookdale in 1803 and a year later, and more famously, at Penydarren colliery.

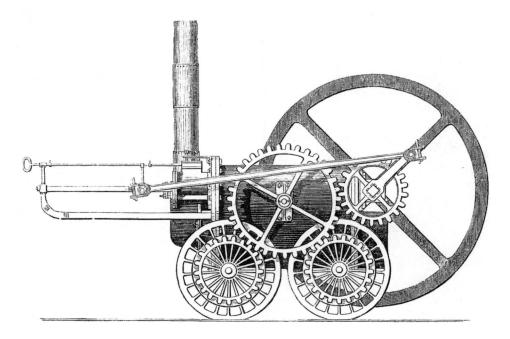

But then railways ought to be safer, for they are far more highly regulated than roads. The very nature of trains – with flanged wheels running on rails – should ensure that they are guided in the right direction and do not veer into each other's path, while signalling also acts to keep trains safely apart, nowadays with a high degree of automation so that human error has become a negligible factor. Even from the earliest days there has been a regime of rules and regulations for staff so that the working of trains can be made as safe as possible. This compares exceptionally well with the UK's Highway Code, governing car drivers, which relies on the common sense (or otherwise) of drivers and pedestrians.

But, if railways are so safe, how come there is enough material for this book? Alas, as in all walks of life, people on railways are only human, and make mistakes. They assume situations are all right when in fact they are wrong, they make errors of judgment, they may lose concentration and so lapse into carelessness. But there is another thing to be considered: precisely because railways have such a good safety record,

Above: The opening of the Stockton & Darlington Railway in 1825. The UK's first all-purpose railway to use steam locomotives represented a huge technological leap forward and therefore gave rise to great celebrations.

whenever an accident does occur, a great deal of material comes into the public domain, from media reports to official inquiries . . . whose results are often published so that lessons can be learnt. Train accidents are big news, even when there have been few casualties. Road accidents often go barely reported.

Primitive railways

Many railway safety procedures and pieces of equipment have been developed as a direct result of accidents. In the pioneering days of railways, during the first half of the nineteenth century –

the first self-propelled steam locomotive was tried out by Richard Trevithick (1771–1883) in 1803, and such locomotives were gradually introduced on colliery railways over the next 20 years, before the first public railways appeared, the Stockton & Darlington in 1825 and the Liverpool & Manchester in 1830 – the two main problems were a lack of communications and the use of materials which, with hindsight, were often unsuited to the developing railways. But at the time there was nothing else: new developments had to await new technology.

So far as materials were concerned, the prime problem was the use of iron for rails, wheels, axles and bridges. Cast-iron was brittle and not strong enough for rails and bridges, as even such an eminent engineer as Robert Stephenson (1803–1859), son of George Stephenson (1781–1848), found to his cost. Wrought-iron was better, but steel, a development of the second half of the century, was really the material for the future – although, as we shall see, even steel has been involved in track failures and broken axles in more recent times.

The other basic problem at the beginning of the railway era was the lack of any means of instant communication between one place and another. As railways were developed, stations were established at towns and villages, and at junctions where one route diverged from another. But how were staff at one station to know before they sent off a train whether the previous train was a safe distance ahead? We must remember that the trains of the 1830s were going at double or treble the fastest land speeds ever before achieved by mankind, whose progress had until then been limited by the rate at which a horse could gallop. A train was obviously much heavier than a horse-drawn carriage and was going much faster, but in those days its brakes were not much better; often they consisted of little more than wooden brake-blocks wound tightly against the wheels by a handle, so that even from an initial speed of only 40 mph (65 kmh) a train often needed half a mile (800 m) or more in which to stop. So, in the absence of a means whereby one station could tell the next when a train was leaving or, the

other way round, when a train had arrived, the railways adopted the time-interval system. This assumed that the train ahead was proceeding according to schedule; the next train waited for a fixed period (i.e. a time interval – hence the system's name) before being allowed to follow. The person in charge of operations at a station (then called the policeman, since security on the early UK railways closely followed the organization of the Metropolitan Police) signalled to the driver of a subsequent train by hand or by different colour flags whether the line was clear. The usual practice was that, within five minutes after the departure of one train, a 'danger' (red) signal was shown to any following train, whose driver would thereby know to come to a halt; if the gap were greater than five minutes but less than ten minutes, the driver would be shown a 'caution' (green) signal, and the train was allowed to go ahead but only at a reduced speed; if ten minutes had elapsed, the second train was shown a 'clear' (white) signal and could proceed at normal speed.

The electric telegraph

In 1837, shortly after the first railways became operational the physicists William Cooke (1806–1879) and Charles Wheatstone (1802–1875) developed the electric telegraph. This electromagnetic device was operated to deflect a pivoted needle within the display case of the receiving instrument to right or left. Originally the telegraph had a bank of five needles which pointed two at a time to a grid of letters, so that messages could be spelt out. Not long afterwards the instruments were simplified, having fewer needle pointers, and after the development of the Morse code in the 1840s, a single needle swung from side to side to represent dots and dashes; messages could be transmitted very quickly using this code. The electric telegraphs on UK railways were soon adapted to be even simpler: the needle remain pegged to one side or the other or remained upright, thereby indicating 'normal', 'line clear' or 'train on line'. This was the basis of what became known as the block instrument, which told staff the condition of the line between any two stations.

But development of the electric telegraph came, at least in the UK, too late to stop the widespread adoption of the time-interval system, which survived for about 60 years. Some railways did not see the use of the telegraph as a vital aid to train safety. Moreover, mechanical signals gradually took the place of flag or hand signals – at first in the form of rectangular boards or discs turned by levers at the foot of their post, and then in the form of semaphore signals giving indications by the angle of the arm of

Left: Even on the pre-steam industrial railways gravity helped to load wagons with coal – as here at South Hetton colliery.

Above: From the mid-1840s the development of the electric telegraph allowed messages in Morse code to be sent between stations and control centres.

Above right: Early signals to drivers on whether it was safe to proceed were given by policemen using hand or flag signals. Standing to attention and not showing a flag was one way of giving a signal.

the state of the line (horizontal for 'danger', inclined down at 45 degrees for 'caution' and vertically down for 'clear', with the colours of red for 'stop', green for 'caution' and white for 'clear').

Interlocking

At first signals and points were worked individually by levers or handles at the site but, from the 1860s onwards, the signal and points levers at a station or junction were grouped together in a single frame and began to be interlocked by mechanical bars and lock bolts so that, if the points were set for a particular line, only the signal levers for that line could be pulled to 'clear'.

Thus points and signals had to agree: signals for conflicting movements could not be cleared together. Thus was initiated the automation of signalboxes (or interlocking towers as they are called in the USA) to prevent mistakes.

The block system

Once block instruments had been instituted, the section of line between one signalbox and the next became known as a block section. Usually there was a single signalbox at each of the smaller country stations and junctions, while larger city stations might have several. A principle known as the 'absolute-block system' became established: not more than one train was allowed on one line in any block section at any one time. This was effected by signalmen (this term had by now replaced 'policemen'): they sent messages on the block instruments, and by electric bells, as trains entered and left the block sections. Each line had its own set of block instruments for every section. The lineside signals outside the box told the driver whether he had to stop or whether it was safe to proceed.

But the whole system relied on signalmen carrying out the proper procedures and on drivers obeying the signals. And, in the mid-Victorian period, not all railway companies were convinced that money should be spent on such precautions. The Railway Inspectorate, which monitored railway safety in the UK, recommended, implored and cajoled the managements of the railways, but had few powers of enforcement.

Single lines

Single lines have always posed more risks than double ones since trains have to work both ways over one set of rails. In the UK, safety on single lines was originally enhanced by having a man to escort each train over each section. Later the system was automated, at first by the use of a wooden staff, and then, by the turn of the century, derived from patents initially registered by the signalling pioneer Edward Tyer in 1878, by electrical devices – a metal staff, a key token or a small round metal tablet was used. The driver of each train running over a single-line section between passing places had to be in possession of the staff or token for that section; otherwise he was not allowed to proceed.

In other parts of the world different systems were used on single lines. In many countries – particularly in North America but also in continental Europe – the staff system was virtually unknown. Instead, the timetable and train-order system was devised. This involved trains working to the schedules, crossing paths with those going in the other direction either at prescribed stations or at remote passing loops – unless they were running late. The line controller, despatcher or the stationmasters at each end of the single line arranged different crossing points by telegraph (later by telephone), and instructed the drivers verbally or, more normally, by written train order showing any altered arrangements. Extra trains were also dealt with by train orders issued to the crews of both the extra and the regular train.

Left: For over 100 years the mechanical lever frame has been used to control signals and points. This is the large signalbox at Newton Abbot East – although it was closed in 1987, to be replaced with modern power signalling, there are still some which remain in operation today.

Above: By the 1920s power control of signals and points was becoming more widespread. This is the power lever frame at Crewe South installed during the early 1940s. The block telegraph instruments are on the shelf above the levers.

trains and higher speeds. Engineers therefore attempted to devise power-assisted brakes. These were various forms of mechanical brake, but the most promising proposals concerned the use of variations in air pressure, either sucking air out of the system to create a vacuum or pumping air into a reservoir so that the compressed air would operate the brakes. Eventually there were two forms of each stratagem, 'simple' and 'automatic'. All four types had an air pipe that ran through the train, with special couplings at the ends of the carriages so that the pipe could be parted when the coaches were uncoupled from each other or from the locomotive.

The simple forms on their own were lethal. In the vacuum version they relied on the ejector on the engine using steam to suck out the air from the pipe so that the resulting vacuum pulled a piston in the brake cylinder of each coach throughout the train. If for any reason the train pipe had broken – say in a derailment – the requisite vacuum could not be created. Similarly, in a simple compressed-air system, if the brake pipe was broken the compressed air could not get through to the brake cylinders.

The automatic vacuum brake worked the other way round. The brakes were held off by a vacuum in the train pipe and brake cylinders. If the brakes were applied by the driver or guard or if the pipe broke, air was admitted to the system but a vacuum was maintained in the brake cylinder on one side of the piston so that, with air on the other side, the piston moved to apply the brakes. And the US engineer George Westinghouse (1846–1914) devised the automatic compressed-air brake which bears his name. In this case the train pipe and the reservoirs on each coach are charged with compressed air to hold the brakes off. If the driver applies the brake or the pipe breaks, air is let out of the pipe and a valve on each coach sends compressed air from the reservoir to the brake cylinder to apply the brakes.

The compressed-air system, often charged to 75 lb/sq in (5 bar), is inherently the more powerful, since the vacuum system is limited by atmospheric pressure – 14 lb/sq in (1 bar) – and has to rely on much larger brake cylinders to give adequate brake power. Furthermore, the vacuum systems are slower to operate than the compressed-air systems.

Sometimes special tail or rear signals, boards or flags were carried on preceding trains. It was – and indeed, still is, in places where this method of operation survives – essential for everyone to pass and interpret messages correctly.

Power brakes

By the mid-1870s it was obvious that hand brakes, possibly assisted by steam brakes on the engine – or by reversing the engine to help slow down – were not adequate for heavier

Train detection

By the final two decades of the nineteenth century various devices were being developed to detect the presence of trains on a section of line. Track circuits first appeared in the USA in the 1870s. In this device a low electric voltage (from a battery) was fed through an electrically isolated section of rails, with a relay at one end; the presence of metal train wheels on the section caused the current to bypass the relay, which could either operate indicators to show the presence of the train or put locks on signals so that another train was not allowed to enter that section. Track circuits spread to the UK in the 1890s and more widely after the First World War. Today they comprise the core of much modern signalling.

But, at the same time as the pioneer track circuits, there came electromechanical treadles. These were applied in what was known as lock-and-block signalling. Trains had to be proved to have operated a treadle before signals would be either locked or released. This system, which provided a form of automated safety for signalmen, was used on some lines in the UK, mainland Europe and elsewhere.

Armagh and its effects

While many signalling and safety developments have been introduced after accidents, it is fair to say that the major disaster in 1889 at Armagh (see page 25) had by far the greatest effect on future railway operation in the British Isles: it brought much tighter safety regulation than in other countries, and at a much earlier date. The line on which it occurred was still operating under time interval rules, trains had simple vacuum brakes and operating procedures were primitive. The British Parliament was shocked into giving the railway inspectorate powers of compulsion to adopt in particular three features, interlocking of signal and points levers in signalboxes, the adoption of the absolute-block system on passenger lines, and the fitting of passenger trains with automatic continuous

Below: The Armagh runaway train and the collision of 1889 brought much stronger legislation from the UK Parliament on the control and operation of railways, enforcing basic safety procedure. The runaway coaches were smashed to matchwood as the debris was scattered down the embankment.

Above: By the 1960s France and Japan were leading the high speed train race with new types of faster trains running at 150 mph (250 kmh) with cab signalling and automated control to prevent driver error. This is one of the Japanese Bullet trains.

brakes, meaning that the brake had to be continuous right through the train, with a few exceptions.

Automation and add-ons

Since the end of the nineteenth century railway safety has improved worldwide. The basic principles of such improvements were established in the last century in the UK, USA and the countries of mainland Europe, and were introduced elsewhere around the globe largely through the colonial system, either through cultural diffusion or through the straightforward selling of equipment.

In the twentieth century, railway safety has been enhanced by added automation, intended to reduce or eliminate human error. By the end of the first decade of this century in the USA and ten years or so later in the UK and Europe, different colours had been adopted for night-time signals and for new lights-only signals – red for 'danger', yellow for 'caution' and green for 'clear', to avoid drivers falsely reading white streetlights bordering railway property as 'clear' signals. Power-operation of points and signals began to replace mechanical wire and rodding, so that signalboxes could control larger areas. Track

circuits were more widely employed, to obviate signalmen's mistakes, and some signals were controlled automatically by track-circuit operation alone. After the Second World War electric power grew to predominance, and later electronics entered the field, providing increased opportunities for long-distance control of signals 100 miles (160 km) or more away, with track circuits showing the location of trains to the operators in the control centre. Today, computers and modern communications – by wire, ground-based radio, satellite, data transmission over long distances or by induction between track or lineside equipment and trains – provide almost total automation. Levers gave way first to buttons and now to computer keyboards.

As for the train driver, automatic warning systems have been developed to tell him whether he can continue at speed or must slow down for a 'danger' signal ahead. Even today, in many countries, this is the only form of aid given to drivers – if any at all – and the safe running of trains still depends on his observation of signals, his correct interpretation of their meaning and his proper handling of the train thereafter; much is left open to human error. On just a few lines – particularly on high-speed routes in Japan, France, Germany and a few other countries and in the Channel Tunnel – is there total automated supervision of the driver's actions, so that safety systems intervene if he fails to slow down or stop for signals or to conform with speed limits. On the latest in-town metro systems, including London's Docklands Light Railway, trains are driven entirely automatically: there is no human hand on the controls.

So what can go wrong?

Even today, despite those safety devices that have been introduced over the past century or more, many railway routes do not have automation to eliminate human error. Safety standards vary widely from line to line and from country to country. There are still stations and junctions in some countries where interlocking is not provided and points are worked by individual levers. The timetable and train-order system remains the operating method on some routes, with telegraph or telephone links between stations. Germany's worst accident in the past 20 years was on a single line with the block system governed by the timetable and by telephone messages (see page 50). On many lines the skill and knowledge of the driver are all that lie between a safe journey and a high-speed wreck. Other disasters have arisen not through operational mistakes but through natural causes, usually related to severe weather –

although even here one must ask if there is not an element of human error: if a bridge collapses beneath a train, plunging it into a raging torrent, could the engineer not have foreseen the consequences, was the bridge's design right, were the materials of which the bridge was built the correct ones? The Tay Bridge disaster of 1879 (see page 64) brought to light many faults in the bridge's construction. In years past there were further factors. What might have been a straightforward collision or derailment was sometimes made many times worse as wooden-bodied coaches were set alight by burning coal flung from the grate under the locomotive's firebox and then, perhaps, exploded into a fireball as gas escaped from the carriages' lighting system – the gas lighting of carriages did not finally disappear until the 1960s. And what of the steam-hauled train climbing a steep gradient through a tunnel? The engine is overloaded, gets slower and slower and finally stops in the long tunnel. The crew try to draw up the fire to make more steam. No operating or signalling mistake here, but exactly these circumstances caused in 1944 one of Europe's worst rail disasters: over 400 passengers died from fumes and carbon-monoxide poisoning (see page 75).

Safety measures can cut down the number and severity of accidents, but they cannot preclude them entirely – as we shall see in the remainder of this book.

Left: The rescue services couldn't save 11 people who were killed when an Amtrak express collided with a Maryland commuter train on the evening of 17 February 1996.

CHAPTER 2

DISASTERS OF VICTORIAN YEARS

For the first 60 years of commercial UK railway operation, from the 1830s to the 1890s, safety procedures evolved only gradually, mainly because there was little communication, unless the telegraph had been installed, and much operating discipline was based merely on printed instructions and rules. The rail disasters of the Victorian era occurred for various reasons – in some cases even the new technology failed to prevent a major crash and many fatalities. The accidents described in this chapter all occurred in the British Isles, but they could equally well have happened anywhere else in Europe, as there was little difference in operating procedures from one country to the next. In the USA and Canada things were different. The distances involved were much vaster, and the installation of the telegraph soon became part of any new railway construction. Elsewhere – in Africa, for example – railways came much later, and therefore incorporated the improved safety standards that had already been developed in Europe.

Left: When runaway goods wagons loaded with drums of paraffin collided with the Irish Mail at Abergele, not only was the engine wrecked, but nobody in the front four coaches survived the fireball.

Clayton Tunnel collision, 1861

The collision on 25 August 1861 at Clayton Tunnel, just over 1¼ miles (2 km) long on the main line between London and Brighton, was all the more shocking because the electric telegraph had become widely used, and was already employed by some railways to operate the absolute-block system. In fact, telegraph instruments had been installed to operate trains through Clayton Tunnel – they were situated in huts at each end of the tunnel normally occupied by the policemen/ signalmen who signalled to train drivers using flags. However, the directors of the London, Brighton & South Coast Railway (LBSCR), which operated the line, were not convinced of the telegraph's advantages, and would not sanction its widespread use; thus the time-interval system was employed on many of the LBSCR's routes, including much of the Brighton main line.

Three trains were scheduled to leave Brighton on the morning of 25 August 1861, heading for London at 10-minute intervals. In fact, since the first was late, they departed at 08.28, 08.31 and 08.35, as instructed by the Brighton stationmaster; these intervals were far shorter than the minimum five minutes laid down in the rules. At the south end of Clayton Tunnel there was another piece of new technology, a warning signal about 300 yd (275 m) from the tunnel entrance. This was generally operated by lever and wire by the signalman but should have returned automatically to show the 'danger, stop' indication when the wheels of passing trains pressed down a mechanical treadle on the inner edge of the rail.

> As the 10.35 climbed hard on the gradient, its fireman saw the runaway coaches hurtling towards him. The driver applied the brakes, but couldn't stop before the runaways hit his engine.

The telegraph instruments were used to send messages from one end of the tunnel to the other. The first train correctly entered the tunnel under 'clear' signals, but the treadle did not operate to set the warning signal to 'danger'. Just over two minutes later the second train approached the south end of the tunnel; the warning signal still showed 'clear'. The signalman looked on in horror – he had not had the telegraph message to say that the first train was out of the tunnel. He just managed to wave a red flag towards the engine as the second train passed at speed. At that moment, however, he received by telegraph the 'train out' message for the first train, and so he sent the 'train in' message for the second – and he had managed to change his warning signal to show 'danger'. Quite what happened after that on the telegraph is not clear from the inquiry report.

However, we do know that the signalman at the south end asked on the telegraph whether the train was out; he was referring to the second train, but the man at the north end erroneously assumed he meant the first. The man at the south end therefore showed 'clear' signals to the driver of the third train. What the south-end signalman did not know was that the driver of the second train had in fact caught just a glimpse of the red flag as his engine had swept into the tunnel, and had applied what little brake power he could, stopping with the back of his train just over 200 yd (183 m) from the tunnel's southern exit. Wondering why he had been shown a red flag, he made the unlucky decision to reverse his train slowly to find out what was going on.

The third train was not travelling very fast as it went into the tunnel – probably at about 25 mph (40 kmh). Its driver could not have anticipated the trap that the general confusion had set. His engine ploughed into the back coaches of the second train, all of which were lightweight timber-bodied vehicles. These were smashed to matchwood, with the wreckage held in an unnaturally compressed pile by the walls of the tunnel. The compacted debris and the darkness collaborated to ensure that casualties were heavy: 23 passengers were killed and 176 were injured, many seriously, out of a total of 589 in the two trains.

The inspecting officer who chaired the inquiry was severe in his criticisms – less of the signalmen than of the system which let three trains start within seven minutes and provided no proper space-interval control, which a complete telegraph block system would have done. The LBSCR objected strongly to the inspecting officer's recommendations that they should install the absolute-block system, but grudgingly acquiesced in the end.

The Staplehurst derailment, 1865

The South Eastern Railway was one of the more farsighted companies: it installed the block-telegraph system throughout its main line from Charing Cross through Tonbridge to Dover during the 1850s. But, for other communication with men carrying out repairs to the line, it relied on printed notices and on the rule-book, which detailed safety procedures. Any work being carried out which entailed disturbance of the track had to be protected by a flagman standing far enough up the line to allow trains to slow down or stop in time; further to ensure that train drivers were aware of the situation, detonators (which would be exploded by the leading wheels of an oncoming engine) were to be clipped on top of the rails.

On 9 June 1865 the track gang at Staplehurst, between Tonbridge and Ashford, were renewing timber baulks on a low cast-iron bridge over a stream. They had nearly finished renewing the 32 baulks, with just one more to do. The foreman planned to accomplish this final task between the trains due to pass towards London at 14.51 and from London at 16.15. The rules said that the line had to be protected by detonators every 200 yd (183 m) on the approach to the obstructed bridge to a distance of 1000 yd (914 m), where the flagman was to put down two detonators and show a red flag to any approaching train. In fact, the flagman had been set in position by reference to the telegraph poles, which were spaced not by the usual distance but by a mere 50 yd (46 m) or so, and thus he was actually standing only just over 550 yd (500 m) from the bridge; furthermore, he had not put down detonators. To add to the confusion, the foreman had overlooked a train that was not in the regular timetable because it ran to connect with a cross-Channel ferry berthing at Folkestone. The times of the cross-Channel services were governed by the tides, and thus also were the times of the connecting boat-trains to London. These train-times were listed in a special notice, but the foreman had misread the date and thought this particular train was due to pass Headcorn, the next station east of Staplehurst, at 17.20; in fact, it was due two hours earlier.

The foreman's gang had put the last new timber baulk in position but had still to replace two lengths of rail when the boat express was seen approaching, at 50 mph (80 kmh). The driver saw the red flag but, with little more than 500 yd (460 m) to the bridge and only hand and special mechanical brakes on

Opposite: The aftermath of the derailment at Staplehurst in 1865. The Folkestone–London boat-train was wrecked when it ran on to a bridge which was being repaired – and the rails had been removed! Charles Dickens was one of the survivors.

a few coaches, there was no chance of stopping before the engine reached the gap in the track.

Surprisingly, the engine, tender and a luggage van continued upright on the timber baulk. However, the sudden uneven weight broke the cast-iron girder, which fell into the stream, as did five out of the front six passenger coaches, the leading one, still coupled to the front van, being left hanging over the gap. Inevitably there were casualties: 10 passengers were killed and 49 injured.

One of the survivors in that front coach was Charles Dickens (1812–1870), who had been going through his manuscript of *Our Mutual Friend* (1864–5) at the time of the accident; eventually he added a postscript to the book referring to the disaster.

The foreman was held responsible for the accident: it was upheld that he had not properly protected the work.

It was not the best of weeks on the railways. Two days before the Staplehurst accident a similar disaster happened at Rednal, between Shrewsbury and Chester. Here the track gang were lifting and packing fine stones under the wooden sleepers to give a better 'level' to the rails. An excursion train approached at speed. The leading driver of the train's two engines did not see the green 'warning' flag attached to a stake on the lineside about 1100 yd (1000 m) from the work, and neither flagman nor detonators were present. The leading engine was derailed by the lifted track but ran on until it hit points at Rednal Station; there it overturned. The train piled up, four coaches being destroyed and others badly damaged. Two of the enginemen and 11 passengers were killed; 30 were injured.

The Abergele collision and fire, 1868

The North Wales main line between Chester and Holyhead runs very close to the coast and, although for much of its length the line is mainly level, it includes a few humps as the railway skirts the beaches and cuts through the cliffs. One of these is fairly sharp, with a three-mile (5 km) climb west of Abergele to Llysfaen before the line drops through the land surrounding Colwyn Bay.

On 20 August 1868 a goods train running from Crewe to Holyhead around midday was calling at intermediate stations to pick up and set down wagons. Standing instructions laid down minimum times for a goods train to leave a station ahead of an express passenger train, so that the goods train

had long enough to be shunted out of the way at a station further ahead. On this particular day the goods train left Abergele little more than 20 minutes ahead of the Irish Mail express from London Euston to Holyhead. The next sidings were about three miles (5 km) further on, at Llysfaen, Llanddulas, near the top of the sharp climb. Even had the goods train been required to do no more than a simple reversing movement into Llysfaen sidings, leaving clear the main line for the Irish Mail, the margin would still have been perilously close. As it was, the Llysfaen sidings were partly occupied with other wagons, and so there was not enough room to shunt the goods train straight in.

The stationmaster decided – strictly against the rules – to split the goods train and leave the rear part of it on the main line, only the front part being put into the sidings. All told, six wagons and the guard's brake van remained on the main line, held on the steep gradient only by the hand brake in the guard's van. The two wagons next to this van were loaded with drums of paraffin. The goods engine emerged from the sidings with three wagons loaded with timber, and gave them a push that set them rolling towards the wagons standing on the main line. The brakeman, running alongside, tried to get the handbrake lever on the side of the wagon underframe properly pinned down to apply the brakes but was unable to do so, and the timber wagons hit the first standing wagon fairly hard. The impact was sufficient to set the six wagons and the guard's van moving backwards down the gradient towards Abergele.

At the time the main line to Holyhead was worked by the time-interval system (although the telegraph was in the process of being installed). There was no means by which the staff at Abergele could know of the drama going on at Llanddulas. The goods train had left the requisite 20 minutes before the Mail passed by, and so they showed the latter the 'clear' signal.

The handbrake of the goods train's guard's van could not hold the runaway wagons, which were gathering speed just as the Irish Mail had passed Abergele and started the climb towards Llanddulas. The Mail was on a curve entering a cutting when its driver and fireman suddenly saw the runaway wagons hurtling towards them. There was neither chance nor time for them to ameliorate the effects of the collision.

The driver jumped seconds before the impact, but his fireman was not so lucky. There was an almighty crash as the wagons broke up on hitting the front of the oncoming engine. Worse was to follow. The drums of paraffin – almost eight tons of it – were thrown from their wagons and broke up as they hit the engine, tender and leading coaches. Immediately the

Opposite: An artist's impression of the inferno near Abergele after the collision between the Irish mail train and runaway wagons carrying paraffin.

engine and front four coaches erupted in a gigantic fireball as burning coal thrown from the engine grate by the impact ignited the paraffin. Nobody in those front four coaches survived: 32 passengers and the fireman died in the flames. This was the worst accident to that date, in terms of deaths, but would be exceeded later.

While the stationmaster at Llanddulas was criticized for having breached the rules, the London & North Western Railway took a share of the blame because its procedures were inadequate and because it was using the Llysfaen sidings without the inspection and approval of the regulatory authority, the Board of Trade. The following decade would see the development of power brakes. In this instance, a broken casting, part of the brake gear of the guard's van, was found soon afterwards near Llysfaen sidings: it had broken when the timber wagons had been shunted too roughly, the result being that there was nothing to stop the wagons from rolling backwards.

River plunge at Tamworth, 1870

The 1870s were a black period for railway accidents, with numerous collisions showing up the deficiencies of the old operating methods and illustrating the need for the much tighter discipline of the absolute-block system, for the interlocking of signal and points levers and for better, more powerful brakes. Other safety devices were also being developed, but often not until accidents had shown the need for them.

At Tamworth, in the early hours of 4 September 1870, the Irish Mail was involved in another accident; this time the train was running the London-bound service. Tamworth, on the Trent Valley route between Rugby and Stafford, had a four-track layout, the outer tracks being loops off the central main lines and running against the platform faces. The route was still operated under time-interval rules, without the benefit of the telegraph. The signalbox controlling the points into the up-platform loop had the home-signal levers interlocked with the points lever; however, the warning signals further out were not interlocked, and these were standing at 'clear'. In fact the points and the home signal were set to divert the train onto the platform loop, because the signalman thought he was expecting a slow goods train; without the telegraph, he had to assume that trains were running as shown in the timetable. To his terror, as he looked through the darkness, he realized that what was approaching was the Irish Mail, travelling fast.

The Mail's driver must have seen the 'clear' signal to the loop line but, with the other signals having been 'clear', had been expecting an unchecked run on the main line. The train was fitted with a patent mechanical brake; this had to be applied by the guards and, with the help of the engine's driving wheels being put into reverse, speed was reduced as the train thundered through the loop. Nevertheless it could not stop before it ran into a siding extension of the loop, crashing through the buffers and down an embankment into the River Tame, into which fell the engine, a mail van and a passenger coach. Surprisingly, casualties were not high: all but the engine crew and one passenger survived. Once again, the lack of proper interlocking and the absolute-block system were highlighted as causes.

Derailment at Wigan, 1873

Within three years of the Tamworth accident, much had changed on the London & North Western Railway: proper absolute-block signalling and interlocking had become standard on its main lines. Wigan Station, on the West Coast main line between Crewe and Preston, had signals and points interlocked, and many expresses passed through every day non-stop at speeds of 40 mph (65 kmh) or even 50 mph (80 kmh).

Right from the dawn of railways there had been a fear of facing points – i.e. points diverging in the direction of travel – in case the switch blades of non-interlocked points could have been set for the wrong direction, so taking a train into danger, notably into the path of another. For this reason sidings were normally connected to main lines by trailing (i.e. converging) points, so that goods trains planning to enter the sidings normally had to go past the points, stop and then reverse in. But, at route junctions and at stations where tracks diverged to serve several platforms, facing points were unavoidable.

At Wigan there were facing points just as the northbound track approached the station, so that two diverging tracks could serve each side of an island platform. The lever was interlocked with the signals to minimize the hazard. Early in the morning of 2 August 1873 an overnight special express of 25 coaches was taking landowners, the affluent and their servants from London to Scotland for their annual visit to the Highlands and the moors. Many of the coaches were saloons occupied by only single families. The express was going through Wigan when, in passing over these points, the sixteenth coach was partly derailed and a luggage van, behind it, totally so. Astonishingly, the two coaches remained coupled

Opposite: The wreckage of the special express from London Euston to the Highlands after several coaches were derailed on points approaching Wigan station in 1873.

Right: The collision near Armagh in 1889 took place on a high embankment, so that debris and the occupants from the wrecked coaches were scattered down its sides.

to those ahead of them. They bounced along the sleepers and ballast and, even more remarkably, were rerailed as they passed through the points at the far end of the platform. The coaches behind them were far less fortunate. There was a scene of utter chaos as some coaches ran up onto the platform, demolishing part of the station roof, and others formed a tangled heap on the track; only the last two coaches remained largely undamaged. Because many of the coaches were carrying only family parties the death toll was not as high as it might have been; even so 13 passengers were killed and 30 injured.

The exact cause was never really ascertained, but one suggestion was that the point switch blades might have moved even though the operating lever in the signalbox was locked; alternatively, the short four- and six-wheeled coaches might have jerked them to the side as they passed through the points. Whatever the truth, the potential for disaster if point blades moved under a train had been made tragically evident, and this led to the introduction of facing-point locks, in which a bolt worked by an extra lever in the signalbox and interlocked with the signals would physically fix the points in the position in which they were set; detectors linked to the blades offered a second line of defence, prohibiting the signal wires from moving if the switch blades were not properly set. Even this equipment was fallible, as was proven at Lichfield in 1946 (see page 66).

The Armagh collision, 1889

On 12 June 1889 a Sunday-school excursion was booked to run at 10.00 from Armagh to Warrenpoint on the east coast of Ireland. The cross-country line linking these two towns was steeply graded in places as it climbed towards the Mourne Mountains: for the first three miles (5 km) out of Armagh it was inclined at 1 in 75. The excursion was expected to be popular, and at the last minute two coaches were added to the train to make a total of 15, all six-wheelers, although only a small 2-4-0 locomotive had been supplied. The train was equipped with a simple vacuum brake and, as was the custom on some railways, the carriage doors were locked. The driver, although not happy with the load his small locomotive was being expected to haul, started out at 10.15. The engine indeed proved unable to get to the top of the climb, stopping just a few yards short of the summit. The man in charge of the train decided to split it, so that the engine could take the front five coaches on to the next station and park them in a siding, then return for the remaining coaches. The handbrakes were screwed on in the back guard's brake van and stones were put under the wheels; the couplings between the fifth and sixth coaches were parted, the disconnection also including the brake pipes – which meant that the back coaches had no power brake available. The engine started to pull forward, but must have gone backwards for just a few inches before the steam pressed on its pistons to get it going. This tiny backward lurch was enough to spell disaster. The buffers of the fifth coach pushed against those of the sixth, and the rear 10 coaches started to roll back, crushing the stones under their wheels as they went. The guard's handbrake could not hold the weight of 10 coaches crammed full of passengers on the steep gradient. The coaches soon gathered speed, running back towards Armagh.

The time-interval system was still used on the line. Since the requisite period had elapsed, the 10.35 train was sent away by the Armagh staff, who obviously had no knowledge of what had happened to the first train. As the 10.35 climbed hard on the gradient, its fireman saw the runaway coaches hurtling towards him. The driver applied the brakes, but had not quite stopped when the runaways hit his engine at about 40 mph (65 kmh), smashing the guard's van – full of standing passengers – and two coaches into matchwood. Then the tender and coaches of the 10.35 became uncoupled and the vacuum brake became ineffective. They too started to run back, but fortunately were stopped by the driver, who had leapt onto the tender and applied its handbrake.

Inevitably, casualties were high: 80 passengers died, including 22 children, and over 260 were injured. The Armagh collision was, in terms of fatalities, the worst accident until then in the British Isles, a macabre record it held for the next 26 years. It spurred the UK Parliament into passing the Regulation of Railways Act (1889), which gave the Railway Inspectorate powers to enforce the installation of the absolute-block system on passenger lines, interlocking of signal and points levers in signalboxes, and automatic continuous brakes on passenger trains. These measures put safety standards on UK railways well ahead of those in other countries. Even today some lines in Western Europe and elsewhere, despite recent developments in automation and communication, still have a few stations, mostly on lightly used branches or cross-country lines, with hand-worked points that lack interlocking, and some lines still rely on the timetable and train-order system, worked in conjunction with telephone or radio communication – or possibly even the telegraph.

OUTCOME

The Armagh accident caused the British Houses of Parliament to pass the Regulation of Railways Act in 1889, tightening railway safety.

CHAPTER 3

MISTAKES BY DRIVERS AND ENGINEERS

So that trains can run safely, the signalman (or despatcher) is responsible for setting the points and ensuring the line is clear. He must carry out his duties correctly and give the proper signals to the driver. Thereafter it is up to the driver to interpret those signals correctly and to control his train to run at the proper speed in all conditions and at all stages of his journey. Here, we look at some of the disasters caused by drivers making mistakes by ignoring or not acting on signals, or by train crews not carrying out instructions in other ways.

Collision at Kentwood, Louisiana, 1903

Left: A mistake by a driver in not seeing a warning signal led to the collision at Lewisham, London, in 1957. The disaster was made worse when the tender damaged a bridge support and the massive girder bridge collapsed on to the coaches below, crushing them.

The newspaper train escaped disaster by inches, or even less. Some of the paintwork of its last coach was scraped, and bits of wreckage flew into the guard's van.

Although the electric telegraph had been developed in the 1840s and demonstrated for railway use a decade later, its general adoption in the USA, even on single lines, was slow: railway managements were reluctant to pay for the innovation. If the telegraph had not yet been installed where trains followed one another in the same direction on double lines (and even on single lines) the time-interval system was used: this system lasted much longer in the USA than in the UK. But, if a train stopped out of course for any reason – shortage of steam, breakdown, etc. – it was essential for one of the train crew, usually the conductor or brakeman, to walk or run back a mile (1.6 km) to protect a standing train by showing a 'danger' signal – holding a red flag or a lamp or both arms raised above the head (as in the UK), putting down detonators on the rails, or letting off flares.

With time-interval working it was quite possible for a following train to be running fairly close behind another, and it was essential for the protection of a standing train to be carried out quickly. But at Kentwood, on the Illinois Central Railroad on

14 November 1903, the crew of a standing train did not go back and protect their train. The following train charged into the back of it, killing 32 passengers and injuring many others. Although this was an accident on a line without the absolute-block system, further protection of a train stopped out of course was necessary, even with the block system, as we shall see.

Collision at Ais Gill, 1913

The Midland main line from Leeds to Carlisle in Northern England running through the Pennines and climbing to a maximum height above sea-level of about 1100 ft (335 m) has always been hard on the operators, for it is often covered in mist or low cloud, perhaps with heavy rain and strong winds; when temperatures fall the conditions can easily turn to sleet and snow. The Midland Railway did not believe in big engines, and ran most of its traffic using small 4-4-0s, although two engines were employed on the heaviest trains, especially over the Settle & Carlisle route, which ran across the Pennines.

On the morning of 2 September 1913 two overnight trains from Scotland to London St Pancras were scheduled to leave Carlisle at 01.35 (from Glasgow) and at 01.49 (from Inverness). The first was well loaded, with 10 coaches, three of them heavy sleeping-cars, the total weight being 13 tons more than was allowed for a single 4-4-0. However, no extra engine was available: the single locomotive had to cope as best it could. There was an added complication: the coal included small lumps

Above: The remains of some of the coaches after the Ais Gill collision in 1913.

order to fill up the oil reservoirs. He was doing exactly this, hanging onto the handrail in the wind and rain, as the train went into Birkett Tunnel about a mile (1.6 km) before Mallerstang. When the train left the tunnel the driver caught a glimpse of Mallerstang distant signal, which he thought showed 'clear'; in fact, all Mallerstang's signals showed 'danger' for the 01.49 train precisely because the 01.35 had not yet cleared the section to Ais Gill. The driver returned to the cab to find the water-level in the boiler very low and that his fireman could not get the water injectors to work properly.

The 01.49 swept by the Mallerstang danger signals and continued towards Ais Gill. The guards of the 01.35 heard the oncoming train and in the dark tried to run back showing a red light and putting down detonators. It was too late. The engine of the 01.49 ploughed into the back coaches of the 01.35. Escaping gas from the lighting system of the coaches burst into flames as a result of red-hot coal from the engine firebox. In the inferno which followed 14 passengers in the sleeping-car, third from the back of the 01.35, were killed.

The Ais Gill disaster, the second major accident to have occurred on this line within a couple of miles (3 km) in three years, resulted in a number of recommendations being made. These included the provision of detonator-placing levers in signalboxes, the use of coloured flares for guards in cases of emergency (this notion was never taken up) and further trials of the automatic train-control system whereby audible indications would be given to the engine cab concerning the position of distant (warning) signals. Known today as the automatic warning system (AWS), this system was already being adopted by the Great Western Railway. Apart from the recommendations, however, there was criticism of the 01.35's crew for not protecting the train and of the 01.49's enginemen for not observing the signals correctly.

Collision at Norton Fitzwarren, 1940

But the AWS system was not foolproof if the driver acknowledged a 'caution' warning but failed to slow down. The equipment on the engine gave audible sounds of the indications shown by a distant signal – in the Great Western type, a horn for 'caution' and a bell for 'clear'. The horn sounded when the engine passed over a track ramp approaching or alongside a distant signal at 'caution', and the brakes were applied automatically unless the driver acknowledged the warning horn by operating a cancelling lever (today's equivalent

and dust and would not give a good hot fire. Just to add to it all, the night was wet, with a strong wind.

The 01.35 train got away, but once it was on the 48-mile (77 km) climb to Ais Gill the steaming got worse, speed dropped and eventually, after the train had passed Mallerstang by about three miles (5 km), stopped just before the summit as the low steam pressure could no longer maintain the vacuum pressure in the brake system. The enginemen set about drawing up the fire to revive the steam pressure and thought this would take only a few minutes; the guards therefore did not immediately go back to protect the train with lamps and detonators.

The second train was doing a little better. Its engine was not fitted with mechanical lubrication, so the driver had to climb out alongside the cab, onto the footplating above the wheels, in

is the pressing of a plunger). The driver was then free to take charge of braking as he thought fit.

But on 4 November 1940 at Norton Fitzwarren, two miles (3 km) west of Taunton on the GWR's West of England route, the driver of an overnight train from London Paddington cancelled the AWS warning as he neared the station. His train was on the down relief line; on his right was the down main line, whose signals were at 'clear' for a newspaper train. Just beyond the platforms the two tracks merged, with a trap point taking the relief line into a dead-end, with soft ground beyond. The relief-line signals were at 'danger', but somehow the driver thought the 'clear' signals he saw were for him. He realized his mistake only as the newspaper train gradually overtook him on the right. The two trains passed through the station together, the newspaper train running fast and the passenger train now

braking hard, but rapidly running out of track as the trap points led it to the dead-end. The big King-class engine tipped into the soft ground and six coaches piled up behind, spreadeagled across all the tracks. As this was wartime, the train was crowded with service personnel. Casualties were heavy: out of an estimated 900 passengers, 27 were killed and 75 injured.

The newspaper train escaped disaster literally by inches, or even less. Some of the paintwork of its last coach was scraped, and bits of wreckage flew into the guard's van as the stricken coaches of the passenger train flew across the tracks immediately behind.

The passenger train's driver was at fault but, what with the difficulties of working in the blackout and the fact that his house had been damaged by bombing two days earlier, criticism was sparing.

Above: Debris from the Ais Gill collision still littered the lineside after the track had been repaired and the trains had resumed operation.

Collisions at Richmond Hill, New York State, 1950, and at Stratford, London, 1953

Suburban and Metro lines, normally working with electric multiple-unit (EMU) trains running services every few minutes, were among the first to have automatic signals. Usually these were colour-light signals controlled by the trains themselves to occupy and clear track circuits. Thus, except at controlled junctions, no signalman was involved. If a signal failed to clear because of a fault – as distinct from there being a train ahead – there had to be some means of keeping the trains moving, as otherwise the entire service could be stopped by, for example, something so elementary as a sticking relay. So the 'stop and proceed' practice was devised for many Metro lines: if trains had to stop at a red signal they were allowed after one minute to pass it and go forward at reduced speed, ready to stop if there was a train ahead or if the driver saw any obstruction. Metal objects thrown across the rails by vandals or a broken rail can be detected by a track circuit, and usually cause the signal for that section to go to 'danger'. Sometimes, if the line is equipped with train stops (preventing a train from running past a 'danger' signal by operating a trip lever on the train to apply the brakes), the driver has to reset a trip arm before proceeding; even so, it is essential that the driver proceeds cautiously, ready to stop on sight. And that is the drawback of the system: too many accidents have been caused by drivers running too fast.

On New York State's Long Island Line on 22 November 1950 a 12-car electric multiple-unit train stopped near Richmond Hill in darkness; the driver, who had slowed for a signal, could not release the brakes. The next signal behind was showing 'stop and proceed' to the following train, so in theory there was no need for the train conductor or his assistant to go back the full braking distance to protect the train – the rules stipulated that a train going forward under 'stop and proceed' should not exceed 15 mph (24 kmh) until it reached the next signal showing 'clear'. In this instance, as the conductor of the standing train thought it was ready to go he jumped back on. It was at that moment that he saw the headlights of the following train, which was travelling at about 35 mph (56 kmh). He immediately turned his red lamp towards it, but there was no chance of the train stopping in time. Nearly 80 passengers were killed and 352 injured in this collision, one of the worst disasters on an urban line in a 'stop and proceed' operation. The driver of the second

train was killed in the accident, so it was never established why he was not running at 'caution'.

On 8 April 1953 at Stratford, on London Transport's Central Line, a trackside train trip arm was damaged by a chain dangling from a train. Its associated signal, and the one behind at Stratford Station, thus remained at 'danger'. From the open-air platforms at Stratford the Central Line towards Leytonstone ran downhill into the tube tunnel, so that drivers went from daylight into the darkness of the tunnel. 'Stop and proceed' working was thus put into operation at Stratford, trains having to wait one minute at the red signal before moving slowly forward. They were then tripped by the train stop. Next the driver would reset the trip arm and restart slowly down to the tunnel. He would repeat the procedure at the next signal.

Several trains had successfully passed the 'danger' signals using this procedure. The eleventh train had stopped at the signal inside the tunnel, ready to trip past it, when the twelfth train – having passed the Stratford signal – halted close behind. The front train completed the tripping procedure and moved slowly away. The one behind it was just about to draw up to the signal when the thirteenth train, running down the slope into the tunnel, collided heavily into its rear, badly damaging coaches of both trains. Twelve passengers were killed and many others were injured.

The driver of the thirteenth train had not operated at the low speed required. But in those days drivers on London Transport lines were not given a practical test of driving at 'caution', and nor did the rules impose a maximum speed. Actual speed for

Right: A fireman examines the crushed coaches of the Central Line train after the collision in tube tunnels on the London Underground near Stratford in 1953.

Opposite: The leading motor coach of the Bury–Manchester electric train lies tail down into the river, having fallen from the Irk Valley viaduct above after the collision with a steam train in August 1953.

'caution' was left to the driver's discretion, bearing in mind the pertaining conditions.

Collision at Irk Valley Junction, Manchester, 1953

Sometimes accidents are caused by the combined mistakes of different people. In this disaster a train driver passed a signal at 'danger' but, had a signalman kept a proper distance between trains, the accident would probably never have happened.

In 1953 the Irk Valley Junction was situated on a viaduct above the River Irk, on the northern approach to Manchester of the line from Bury; a branch led off to the east, towards other lines and the route to Bacup. Today everything has changed: the branch has gone, and the Bury line is now the main route of Manchester's Metrolink trams.

On 15 August 1953 the signalman at Irk Valley Junction accepted a Bury to Manchester electric train from Queens Road signalbox – the next box on the line from Bury – at 07.29 and, four minutes later, he accepted the 07.36 local steam train from Manchester to Bacup, which was supposed to take the right-hand track at the junction. Absolute-block working was in force in all directions, but all the home ('stop') signals were close to the junction. Normally, before a signalman could accept a train in this sort of working, the line had to be clear for a quarter of a mile (400 m) beyond the home signal, in case a driver misjudged his braking.

The points on the line from Manchester were set towards Bury, so all was well . . . so far. However, the electric train did not come immediately, so the Irk Valley signalman reset the points for the steam train to turn to the right. The diversion was only a few yards beyond the signal from the Bury line – far under the prescribed quarter-mile (400 m) extra clearance. The steam train accelerated to the right-hand track, but almost immediately the electric train appeared from the Bury line. It hit the steam locomotive on its left side and was itself thrown to the right. Its leading coach smashed through the parapet and plunged 40 ft (12 m) to the riverbank below, the back end dropping down the bank another 30 ft (9 m) into the river.

Had it not been a Saturday, the electric train would have had many more passengers; even so, ten people (including the driver) were killed and 58 injured, 22 of them seriously.

The driver of the electric train was blamed for passing a 'danger' signal and the signalman for infringing the quarter-mile (400 m) rule.

Collision at St. Johns, London, 1957

Below: The horrific conditions under the collapsed girder bridge which flattened coaches of the Ramsgate train after the collision at St. Johns, London, in 1957.

Since the mid-1920s the Southern Railway had pressed on with modernization, introducing colour-light signals (a lights only system) and track circuits that allowed some to work automatically and that, on others, provided checks on signalmen's actions. Such measures were the start of the automation that led towards the elimination of signalmen's errors, but on the Southern there was as yet no automation for drivers, who had to look for and obey signals. The main line from Charing Cross to Dover had colour-light signals for its first few miles out of London; even in fog these were very effective, the beams of light being bright enough to penetrate the gloom.

The evening of 4 December 1957 was very foggy in south-east London, and many trains were delayed. Most trains out of

Charing Cross were EMUs, but the main-line trains to Dover and Ramsgate were still steam-hauled. The 16.56 train from Charing Cross to Ramsgate left 45 minutes late amid a thick fog that surrounded New Cross and St. Johns. Normally the driver would have been able to see the signals, some of which were to the right of the line; this evening, however, because of the fog, he missed two in the approach to St. Johns. Both were showing 'caution'.

Suddenly the fireman saw the red signal at the further end of St. Johns Station. He called to the driver to stop, but it was all too late. Only 138 yd (126 m) beyond was the back of an electric train which was waiting for a 'clear' signal. The heavy Battle of Britain 4-6-2 hit the electric train so hard that two coaches were telescoped, one ending up inside the other. Even worse was to come. The steam engine's tender swung to the left and displaced a steel column that supported a massive 350-ton girder bridge which carried other lines. The bridge collapsed onto the wreckage and flattened the leading two coaches of the

Ramsgate train. All told, 90 people were killed and 109 were seriously injured – and all because a driver missed two warning signals. The disaster could have been averted had the automatic warning system been installed by then, but at that time it was not deemed sufficiently reliable for use on Southern Region's electric lines, although cost might also have played a part in the company's decision.

Collisions at Harmelen, 1962, and Schiedam, 1976

The dangers of trains running in both directions towards a junction – even for only a short distance – on a line that is normally used only one-way were graphically illustrated by a head-on collision on the Netherlands Railways Utrecht–Rotterdam line. For a short distance at Harmelen near Woerden, Rotterdam–Amsterdam trains crossed from the eastbound line to the westbound line before turning off the main line. On the foggy morning of 8 January 1962 a six-coach EMU on the Rotterdam–Amsterdam service had just crossed to the westbound track when a Utrecht–Rotterdam express hauled by an electric locomotive missed the distant warning signal and started to brake only as the stop signal came into view. The express was still travelling at over 60 mph (100 kmh) when it hit the EMU head-on. Three coaches of the EMU and six coaches of the express were wrecked; 93 people were killed and hundreds injured in the Netherlands' worst rail disaster.

The accident caused so much consternation that the Dutch authorities started work on not merely an automatic warning system (AWS) but one which would provide much fuller automated control of the driver's actions, to ensure he could not run past a signal at 'danger' and to supervise speed restrictions. This system formed the basis of what we know today as automatic train protection (ATP). Nevertheless, as many as 14 years later in the Rotterdam suburbs a similar accident occurred. The Rhine Express from Hook of Holland was switched to the left-hand track near Schiedam to overtake a stopping train making a call. Both lines were signalled for reversible working. An EMU coming in the opposite direction ran past a 'danger' signal onto the northbound Hook of Holland line. It went into the Rhine Express head-on and the resulting wreck involved all three trains, 24 people losing their lives. Installation of ATP had been carried out on about a quarter of the Dutch network by then, but not on this line. The disaster helped to speed up further installation. Today most lines in Holland are fitted with ATP.

Left: Rescue workers pick their way through the twisted metal in the wreckage of the two trains involved in the Harmelen head-on collision.

Below: The aftermath of the Schiedam collision between a locomotive-hauled train on the right of the picture and a multiple unit. After this accident the Dutch authorities speeded up work on an automated system to prevent driver error.

CHAPTER 4

OPERATIONAL MISTAKES

Once signalboxes (interlocking towers) had become established, from the 1860s onwards, and the block system had been developed in conjunction with the telegraph, railway operation became much more disciplined: fairly precise rules and regulations were laid down regarding the procedure to be adopted for train signalling and movement authorization. Although the beginnings of signal automation dated back to the mid-1870s, with the invention of lock-and-block systems and track circuits, it took another 25 years for such equipment to be refined into reliable form for wider use, railway managements being slow to adopt them. They cost money, and too many senior railway managers were more concerned with costs than with safety. At most signalboxes strict observance of rules and regulations was the norm, rather than automated safety add-ons.

Quintinshill, 1915

Left: Breakdown gangs clearing the wreckage after the 1948 Winsford collision when the Night Mail from Scotland, the engine of which is just behind the coach in the foreground, ran into a train stopped when the alarm signal was operated.

The troop train did not stand a chance. It was travelling fast downhill. . . . Its engine hit the engine of the local train head-on, and many of its 21 coaches became a pile of wreckage. . . .

In 1923, in the days before the railways were grouped into four big companies, over 100 railway companies ran the UK's railways. Sometimes two or more different railways ran their own parts of what were logically single through routes. The main line from London Euston to Glasgow Central, the West Coast route, was split in two, with the LNWR operating from London to Carlisle and the Caledonian from Carlisle to Glasgow. Just two miles (3 km) into Scotland from the English border was a remote signalbox at Quintinshill. There was no station: just a double-track main line plus extra loop tracks on the outside, one for northbound trains and one for southbound. In 1915, early in the First World War, there were many extra trains carrying men and materials to the UK's ports.

On 22 May 1915 a special troop train was booked to run from Larbert to Liverpool. At 06.00 the night signalman was due to hand over to the early-turn man, but the latter did not arrive until 06.30. The early-turn signalman travelled to work on a local passenger train from Gretna, the next station to the south. On this particular morning the train was, to keep it as near to the timetable as possible, sent away from Carlisle ahead of two late-running overnight expresses from London (one for Edinburgh and beyond and the other for Glasgow). The plan was that the local train would be switched off the main line at Quintinshill. As luck had it, there was heavy goods traffic, and so the down-loop at Quintishill was occupied by a goods train waiting to continue north. At the same time, a train of empty coal wagons was entering the up-loop to wait until it could continue to Carlisle. The only way the local passenger train could get out of the way of the overnight expresses was to reverse to the up main line. The early-turn signalman took over the control of the signalbox and started writing up the register of block signalling times after 06.00 to cover up the fact that he should have been on duty but had been late. There were other people in the signalbox, some from the crews of the two goods trains, plus the fireman of the local train; he signed the register to say his train was standing on the up-line. He acted in accordance with Rule 55 of the rulebook, devised to remind signalmen that a train was standing on a running line. However, its 21 coaches – largely old gaslit six-wheelers, packed with soldiers – became a pile of wreckage compressed to less than a quarter of its original length. The railwaymen in the signalbox looked on aghast as tragedy unfolded, then suddenly realized the signals were 'clear' for the first of the overnight expresses from London, fast approaching and only about a quarter of a mile (400 m) away. Although they tried to warn it, the two engines hauling the heavy express had hardly slowed when they ploughed into the debris of the first collision. White-hot coal was flung from the firebox and, with gas escaping from the ruptured pipes of the lighting of the old coaches, an inferno soon broke out. The whole pile burst into flame: the blaze did not die down for 24 hours.

In the carnage at Quintinshill 227 are known to have died, and nearly 200 passengers were injured – exact numbers have never been determined, because the military records were likewise lost in the fire. The two signalmen took the blame as a result of their inattention and their failure to carry out the rules. They were convicted of manslaughter and served prison terms. Although the inquiry report was less critical than it might have been – because of war conditions – the signalmen were in fact not entirely at fault: the technology that could have prevented the accident, in the form of track circuits, was by then available to the railway owners . . . had they been willing to pay for it.

Collision at Batignolles Tunnel, Paris, 1921

The main line west from Gare St Lazare in Paris not only carried long-distance trains to the north-west of France but also frequent suburban trains to the west of Paris. For many years operation was hampered by a tunnel about half a mile (1 km) in length at Batignolles, just outside St Lazare Station: the presence of the tunnel limited the number of tracks that could be laid down. Just as at Quintinshill, the dangers of gas lighting in an accident were amply shown up in a collision on 5 October 1921 when a local train for Versailles stopped in the tunnel. The signalmen at each end of the tunnel inadvertently subverted the block system, and a second train was allowed to proceed, colliding with the back of the first. There were casualties from the collision, and then fire broke out because of escaping gas. The official death toll was 28 but, since nobody knew for certain how many passengers were travelling on the two trains, the figure was undoubtedly higher.

The French authorities immediately set about replacing all remaining gas lighting in coaches by electricity, but it would

Below: The memorial parade for the servicemen killed in the Quintinshill collision in 1915.

the fireman failed to check that the signalman put reminder collars on the lever of the signal protecting the train.

Since the local train was standing on the up-line, the signalman should also have sent a special bell signal to Kirkpatrick, the next signalbox to the north, to stop any up-trains there. As a consequence, Kirkpatrick offered the troop train to Quintinshill, where the early-turn signalman not only accepted it but had it accepted by Gretna; he also cleared all the signals for it at Quintinshill, even though the up-line was obstructed, directly outside the signalbox, by the local train.

The troop train did not stand a chance. It was travelling fast downhill from Beattock summit, high on the Southern Uplands. Its engine hit the engine of the local train head-on, and many of

OUTCOME

Batignolles tunnel was opened out to allow additional tracks rather than the two. The signalmen were jailed for their actions.

Right: The head-on collision just north of Bellinzona in 1924 when four electric locomotives, two on each train, met head-on when one train failed to stop at a signal and was diverted into the path of the other.

take several more years and several more fires before gas was eliminated. In the UK most gaslit coaches were gone by the 1950s, but a few survived even into the 1960s, notably on a Devon branch line (on this line propane gas had to be used because speeds were too low for the batteries of electrically lit coaches to be charged by the generators driven by the wheels).

As with the disaster at Quintinshill, the two signalmen at Batignolles were jailed for their actions. The tunnel was opened out shortly afterwards so that more tracks could be laid.

Collision at Bellinzona, Switzerland, 1924

A gaslit coach added to the casualties in a head-on collision between two electrically hauled passenger trains at Bellinzona on the Gotthard main line in southern Switzerland in the early hours of 23 April 1924. Much of the internationally famous Gotthard route, which linked France and Germany with Italy and passed through the Alps via the 9¹/4-mile (15km) Gotthard Tunnel, had a double track. As it approached Bellinzona Station from the north, descending from

the Gotthard Tunnel, the line had additional tracks on the west side; these served San Paola goods station. A series of crossovers allowed southbound goods trains heading for San Paola to diverge rightwards across the northbound main line and onto the goods lines. But at the time control of the points and signals was only temporary: the station was being reconstructed. A notable omission was the lack of interlocking between the points levers and some of the signals. Just before the points that diverted trains to the goods lines was a stop signal; further on, another signal governed entry to the passenger station.

The pointsman responsible for controlling moves into the goods station from the main line was expecting a goods train from the north, and thus he left the points set from the southbound main line, so that the train could go across the northbound line towards the goods tracks. But his signal on the main line was set at 'danger', to stop an approaching train. Unknown to him the goods train was running late, and had been overtaken by an express from Basel and Zurich (bound for Chiasso): no advice of the trains being out of order had been transmitted to him. Meanwhile, from the south, a late-running express from Milan to Dortmund was leaving Bellinzona ready for the climb to the Gotthard Tunnel. Like the southbound express, it was hauled by two electric locomotives. The pointsman, in the general confusion, forgot that his points were set towards the goods line. When he saw the southbound express approaching he left his signal at 'danger' but, to his horror, he saw that the train was not stopping. The two locomotives swung to the right, so meeting the northbound train head-on at the intersection.

Both trains had heating vans immediately behind their locomotives; these were designed to provide steam heat to the passenger coaches as most trains were steam-hauled once beyond the Swiss frontier. The heating vans absorbed some of the impact. Nevertheless, damage to the northbound express was severe, the first two passenger carriages being badly damaged. The leading passenger carriage from Germany, was unfortunately gaslit and became a fireball – probably because the escaping gas was ignited by fire from the train's heating-van boiler or by sparks from the overhead electrical catenary that powered the locomotives.

All told, 15 people died in the accident, which had two primary causes. Firstly the southbound express's driver deliberately went past the 'danger' signal, thinking it applied only to goods trains. The other cause was the incorrect setting of the facing points and lack of interlocking with the northbound signals. Soon after, the Swiss banned all gaslit coaches and there were calls for the introduction of the advance-warning system (AWS).

Collision at Hull Paragon, 1927

In the UK interlocking had been compulsory on passenger lines for nearly 40 years, so a Bellinzona-type accident could not, in theory, occur . . . or could it? On the approaches to Hull Paragon Station on the misty morning of 14 February 1927 an outgoing train from Hull to Scarborough was accelerating on its proper line, line C, with signals showing 'clear'. Ahead of it was a series of points crossing from incoming line B (on its right) to incoming line D (on its left), with point switches on line C to allow an incoming train to cross from line B to C. For the signal to show 'clear' straight ahead on line C for the outward-bound train the points had to be set straight ahead along line C, and locked in that position.

But somehow, the outgoing train was switched from line C over the crossover to line B. Just as the driver realized he was on the wrong line, his train was hit head-on by an incoming train from Withernsea, which had indeed been scheduled to arrive on line B and then was later switched to line D.

The impact was fierce, and several of the old wooden coaches either telescoped through each other or broke up. Though the engine crews survived, 12 passengers were killed. Since full interlocking was in place, how could this accident have happened? The inspecting officer who chaired the inquiry had a puzzle on his hands.

Left: Force met force when incoming and outgoing trains collided head-on outside Hull Paragon in 1927. They locked chimney to chimney all because a signalman pulled the points lever too quickly.

Above: Two coaches on surburban electric trains were virtually destroyed in the 1937 Battersea Park collision caused when a signalman mistakenly overrode safety locking equipment.

to set the points for the incoming train. Intending to pull lever 96, so that the incoming train would be held until the Scarborough train had cleared the points, in his haste he accidentally pulled lever 95 instead. At that moment only a few seconds remained before the front wheels of the engine reached the locking bar, which would have prevented the points from moving. It was too late: the locking bar moved and the facing point lock was unbolted. The points changed to switch the outgoing train from line C to B, and thus towards the incoming train.

Both signalmen were blamed for not observing the rule defining when a signal should be restored to 'danger', but if a track circuit had been placed on the approach to the points the accident would have been prevented.

Collision at Welwyn Garden City, 1935

There was another puzzle to sort out after a massive collision between following express trains at Welwyn Garden City on the main line from London King's Cross to the north late on the night of 15 June 1935. The signalbox here had six tracks to control: the four tracks of the main line plus a branch on each side. There were 16 block instrument indicators and associated bells. Three express trains left London in quick succession, the 22.45 for Newcastle, the 22.53 for Newcastle and the 22.58 for Leeds.

The 22.45 passed Welwyn correctly and continued on its journey, but for some reason the signalman did not clear the signals for the following 22.53. It passed the distant signal for Welwyn at 'caution' and slowed down, the driver assuming he was catching up with the first train and thus would have to stop somewhere ahead. As he approached the station, the signals were changed to 'clear' but, a minute or so later, as he accelerated, his train was rammed from behind by the 22.58, which was travelling at about 70 mph (115 kmh). The back coach of the 22.53 was demolished and others were damaged, while two coaches of the 22.58 were telescoped – although several of its coaches had centre buck-eye knuckle couplers (an alternative to side buffers and link couplings) and thus held firm and in line. Casualties were heavy: 13 passengers died and 81 were injured.

How had it happened that the 22.58 train had entered the section from Hatfield while the 22.53 was still in the section and running slowly?

The inspecting officer concluded that the inexperienced signalman had become confused, wrongly clearing the down-line block instruments for an up-train and not realizing that,

Park Street signalbox, which controlled this part of the line, had 179 levers and was worked by two men. The signal for the outgoing train was worked by lever 171 which, when pulled to 'clear', locked the points on line C (worked by lever 95) in their straight-ahead position. Next to 95 was, obviously, lever 96; this worked the points for the crossing move from line B to line D. As the outgoing train approached the points one signalman put signal lever 171 back to 'danger' while the third coach was passing it; the driver thus saw the signal as 'clear'. The signalman's action released the interlocking on levers 95 and 96. The second signalman was anxious to save time, and so started when he accepted the 22.58, the 22.53 had still to reach him. The officer recommended that two track circuits should be connected to the block instruments and the signal levers in such a way that a train must be proved to have passed all the way through a block section, with the signals replaced to 'danger' behind it before the block instruments could be cleared for another train. This became mechanical signalling's ultimate in block protection, and was accordingly called Welwyn control. The system survives today, although it has not been installed everywhere.

Collisions at Battersea Park, 1937, and South Croydon, 1947

Over 50 years earlier, another form of block protection had been developed to establish much the same safety procedures as the Welwyn control. This was named the Sykes lock-and-block system, after its inventor, and it was used on many lines south of London, on some in east London and in a few other places. Treadles were set alongside the rails, and the passing of train wheels sent electrical signals to the signalbox equipment, where they powered or released electrical locks on the block instruments and signal levers. Before a signal could be cleared for a train, the block instrument for the section ahead had to show 'free'; once the next train had gone forward the section was locked until the train had passed out of the far end of that section. Occasionally, however, a faulty contact failed to clear a lock; to avoid stopping the entire service, the signalmen then had to use a release key or plunger to bypass the locks (usually only with the cooperative action of the adjacent signalbox). This ability to override was the system's downfall, since it led to several accidents when signalmen thought, wrongly, the equipment had failed.

On the morning of 2 April 1937 at Battersea Park, on the main line approaching London Victoria from Brighton, the signalman, a relief man who had only recently been passed to work there, got into difficulties as he tried to clear a signal from the South London line before changing the points. The Sykes equipment locked the system up, and he attempted to use the release plunger to allow another attempt at changing the points . . . but again he had no success. Meanwhile, a train from London Bridge had arrived at his up local line home signal, where it was held at 'danger' by the Sykes locking through the junction points, connecting with the South London line.

The signalman cut the seals on the locking box to try to get his hand inside and release the lock manually. Whether he succeeded or not, the block-instrument locking for the section from Pouparts Junction, the next signalbox away from London, became free for the up local line. The Pouparts Junction signalman thought he had clearance to send forward a train from Coulsdon to Victoria. In the fog, its driver saw the standing London Bridge train only when he was within about 50 yd (46 m) of it, and could not avoid a collision. The front coach of the Coulsdon train and the rear coach of the other were wrecked; 10 passengers were killed and 80 injured – astonishingly, the driver of the Coulsdon train, even though his cab had been demolished around him, was only slightly injured. The signalman had to accept the blame for his actions.

A decade later, on 24 October 1947, another accident on the Southern line came about through mishandling of the Sykes system. This was at South Croydon, also on the Brighton main line.

Left: At South Croydon, 10 years after the Battersea Park tragedy, another signalman also bypassed safety locking equipment and caused a collision between two electric trains in thick fog, killing over 30 people including the driver of the second train.

RECOMMENDATIONS

The outcome of the Welwyn disaster was the provision of a new block instrument/signal locking system – known as the Welwyn control.

Smog was a regular feature of suburban London in cold, still, damp weather – often it was caused by the use of so many coal fires in the days when domestic central heating was little known. During the morning rush-hour on this calamitous day the commuters and railway operators had to contend with a very thick smog. Drivers had to take their trains at no more than a crawl up to signals to check they were not at 'danger' unless they had passed a 'clear' distant signal, and signalmen could not see trains even 50 yd (46 m) away.

At Purley Oaks, the station immediately south of South Croydon, the signalman had sent an electric train from Haywards Heath to London Bridge forward to his starting signal, set at 'danger' because the line was not yet clear to South Croydon. Then, alas, he forgot about it. As it had not passed over the treadle to free the block section behind it from Purley, this was correctly still locked to prevent the approach of another train. However, the signalman at Purley, the next box along, had further trains to send forward, and so he telephoned to Purley Oaks to ask when the line would be free. The Purley Oaks man tried to clear the block indicator, found it locked, and used the release key to free it.

He accepted a following Tattenham Corner–London Bridge train from Purley and, as the line to South Croydon was by then clear, signalled it forward. The Haywards Heath train moved forwards but the Tattenham Corner one was travelling faster with all signals showing 'clear', and collided with it at South Croydon. The front coach of the Tattenham Corner train was wooden-bodied and was totally destroyed. All told, the driver and 31 passengers were killed and many of the 1800 passengers on the two trains were injured – all because an inexperienced signalman thoughtlessly used the Sykes release key.

Collision at Winsford, 1948

The origin of the events leading to the disaster at Winsford, on the flat Cheshire Plain north of Crewe, a few minutes after midnight on 16 April 1948, was not of the railway's own making. The sequence started when a soldier travelling on the overnight 17.40 Glasgow to London Euston train pulled the communication cord (alarm signal) near Winsford. He lived nearby and, by hopping off the train as it came to an emergency stop here, he could save himself some time since he would not have to go all the way into Crewe and then catch a local train back out again. The railways have rules and regulations to ensure the safety of trains brought to an emergency halt, but they did not work that night.

The guard and fireman walked the length of the train to try to find out why the train had been stopped and to see in which coach the alarm signal had been operated. Their chore was not going to be a quick one, and so the train should have been protected with detonators and a red light. It should have been further protected by the signalling system but, alas, when the signalman at Winsford Junction telephoned to Winsford Station signalbox to ask about the delay, the man at Winsford Station thought he must simply have missed seeing the Glasgow–Euston train go past. He therefore wrongly cleared the block instruments for the section from Winsford Junction, and accepted the following train – the Night Mail from Scotland to London, composed entirely of mail carriages in which postmen were sorting the letters.

The guard of the 17.40 train eventually decided to protect his train, but too late. He had gone no more than about 400 yd (365 m) back from it and was just about to put a detonator on the rail when the heavy Night Mail sped past him and thundered into the rear of the standing passenger train. The impact was so severe that the back five coaches of the passenger train and the front five mail coaches were badly damaged or destroyed, with 24 people being killed and many injured.

Collision at Stechford, Birmingham, 1967

By 1967 modern signalling – with full track circuiting, colour-light signals and centralized control – had been installed in the Birmingham area, but goods yards and their connections with the main lines were often controlled locally by special shunting signalboxes, with electrical or electronic locks being released from the main signalbox. This was the situation at Stechford, to the south-east of Birmingham on the main line to London Euston.

Stechford not only served the tracks from Birmingham New Street, but was also the junction with a route known as the Grand Junction line, which bypassed the centre of Birmingham. A northbound ballast train arrived from Coventry, but was too long to shunt into the sidings. It was parked on the Grand Junction up-line to allow its diesel locomotive to go forward on the down Grand Junction line and then back in the wrong direction over the main Birmingham down-line, and thus reach the other end of the train. The rules did not allow this, but the shunter was planning to organize things over the telephone with the main Birmingham signalling centre. Before he did so, the shunter waved to the ballast train's guard to call him to the opposite end of the train. Unfortunately, the secondman on the locomotive standing on the down Grand Junction line took the wave as a hand signal to move. The driver opened the controller and the locomotive went towards the down Birmingham line. It reached the crossing with the Birmingham up-line at the same time as an up express electric multiple unit (EMU), running under 'clear' signals. The EMU hit the locomotive with such force that the EMU's coaches were lifted into the air and thrown across to the far side of the Birmingham down-line, sweeping away the overhead gantries that carried the electrification catenary wires. The EMU driver and eight passengers were killed, and 16 others – including railwaymen who had been learning the line – were injured.

This accident occurred because of the use of a banned move and the incautious wave of a hand. It was a most unfortunate inauguration for the new, full electrical services and the modernization of the lines between Liverpool, Manchester, Birmingham and London that was completed only a few days later.

Below: But for an illegal manoeuvre and an incautious wave, the driver of the electric train and 8 of his passengers would have survived. This carriage bears testimony to the force of the collision which scattered carriages across several tracks.

CHAPTER 5

THE DANGERS OF SINGLE LINES

The electric staff/token systems were developed in the UK for single-line signalling; they were used also in some other countries, either UK-administered or where UK companies ran the railways. Elsewhere, once the electric telegraph had been adopted, the timetable and train-order system was employed extensively. Before the advent of the telegraph, however, in many countries nothing other than the timetable and special operating rules governed single-line movements, particularly where there were long distances between passing places, as in North America. Inevitably mistakes occurred, and instructions were misunderstood. Even after the introduction of the telegraph, wrong or incomplete information could be written on train orders, or the orders could be misread by the locomotive crew. The result might well be what has often been referred to in the USA as a 'cornfield meet' – i.e. a head-on collision. This is potentially the worst type of accident involving two trains, even if both are travelling at relatively low speeds, because the impact velocity is the sum of the speeds of the two trains.

Collision at Camp Hill, Pennsylvania, 1856

An example of a major disaster on a US single line in pre-telegraph days was the collision between a local train and an excursion train that was carrying Sunday school children from Philadelphia for a day out and picnic at Fort Washington, about an hour away. The excursion was running on a train order as an extra and, provided it remained on time, would arrive at Fort Washington before the local train to Philadelphia reached there, travelling in the opposite direction. The rules said that, if the special was more than 15 minutes late, it would be shunted off the main line at a siding before Fort Washington, so that the local train could pass. Also, the local train had standing instructions to wait for up to 15 minutes at Fort Washington if the special had not arrived on time. The system seemed foolproof.

The special was indeed 15 minutes late when it reached the siding before Fort Washington. However, knowing that the regular train had instructions to wait 15 minutes, the special's conductor decided to continue. Meanwhile, even though the 15 minutes had yet to elapse, the conductor of the local assumed the special must be waiting for his train to pass, and so he decided to proceed slowly. The local was travelling at only about 10 mph (16 kmh) when its engineer and fireman saw the oncoming special running downhill at 35–40 mph (55–65 kmh). Handbrakes had hardly begun to grip when the two engines met. The carnage was awful. Coaches were not merely smashed to splinters, but erupted into a fire which engulfed half the excursion train. Over 60 passengers died. As a direct consequence, the conductor of the local train later committed suicide. However, the blame for the disaster was placed on the conductor of the special.

Despite the potential for disaster on single lines, many railroads in North America were reluctant to install the

Left: The tangle of mangled steel and smashed timberwork after the Abermule head-on collision in Wales in 1921.

Right: The pile of wreckage after the head-on collision between the up mail train from Yarmouth and the London–Yarmouth express near Brundall in 1874. The collision was caused by staff misunderstandings at Norwich.

telegraph: even if they had the equipment, they often did not use it. The reason was that much the same distrust of new technology and its cost prevailed in high places on some US railways as did in the UK.

It should be emphasized, though, that the telegraph system was merely a safety aid. It was not foolproof, and it relied on all the participants either sending messages correctly or interpreting them correctly. Even in the UK, collisions on single lines controlled by the telegraph were not unknown, although they were rare – mainly because the UK's lines were short by comparison with those in the USA and did not have such heavy traffic.

One of the worst of the UK's single-line disasters occurred near Norwich.

Collision near Norwich, 1874

The single track Norwich–Yarmouth line in East Anglia was one of the earliest in the UK to be equipped throughout with the telegraph. Installed in 1848, the telegraph had provided secure train working until the evening of 10 September 1874. The 17.00 Liverpool Street–Yarmouth express, which had to reverse in Norwich Thorpe, was booked to cross the 20.40 up mail-train from Yarmouth at Brundall. The express was 20 minutes late, and the night inspector suggested to the stationmaster that the mail train should be sent on from Brundall to Norwich. After some discussion, the inspector thought the stationmaster had agreed and so instructed the telegraph clerk to send a message to Brundall to despatch the mail train on its way to Norwich. The inspector did not sign the written note to the clerk, as required by the rules, but the telegraph clerk nevertheless transmitted the message to Brundall.

The tragedy occurred also because the day inspector, about to go off duty, had already given a written order to the express driver to proceed to Brundall, not realizing that the telegraph clerk had ordered up the mail train. Only a minute or two later did all concerned discover what they had done. They had to endure long minutes of horror, knowing they had sent two trains towards each other and were now powerless to stop them. The two trains met at a combined speed of 50–60 mph (80–100 kmh) just yards from the bridge over the River Yare, two miles (3.2 km) from Norwich. Both trains were heavy, one with 14 and the other with 13 four-wheeled coaches. Many of the coaches were destroyed in a mountain of wreckage; 25 people, including both locomotive crews, were killed, and over 70 were injured. The back coaches of the express came to rest on the bridge; it was fortunate that nobody was drowned by falling into the river from the bridge, which had no parapet.

Ironically, work was already in hand to make this part of the line double-track. As for the immediate cause of the disaster, it was really a case of too many cooks: the day and night inspectors did not coordinate their actions and the night inspector and the telegraph clerk did not comply with the regulations over signature of the order for the mail train.

Train order mistakes in North America

The USA had a huge railway mileage operated by the telegraph system, and without any automation to help avoid human error, so it was inevitable that disastrous mistakes occurred. That said, the telegraph system was supplemented by standing instructions, which gave different categories of trains priority over others: lesser trains had to shunt into sidings and wait, trains in one direction were given the right of way over those going in the opposite direction, etc. If the traffic was heavy, some services might be run in two portions, and thus a train waiting in a siding would have to be informed that not one but two trains were coming. The driver of the waiting train would have been given the relevant orders, but often the information was imparted additionally by flag or board signals carried on the first portion of the train that was being given clearance.

The fallibility of this system was displayed at Warrensburg, Missouri, on 10 October 1904. The crew of a freight train waiting in a siding for a booked crossing did not notice the 'extra train' signals on the first express, and started out of the siding onto the single track. The freight train met the second express head-on. Even at the relatively low impact speed of 30 mph (50 kmh) the leading coach was wrecked, and 29 passengers were killed.

On 16 March 1906 the alertness of a telegraph operator at Beaver Station, on the Denver & Rio Grande Railroad, was at fault. In the early hours he was asked by his line despatcher, on the telegraph, whether a westbound express had passed. He had been on duty for much of the previous day and on into the night, and had very briefly dropped off to sleep. As he had dozed, the express had gone through. Unwittingly, he replied to the despatcher that the train had not yet passed. The despatcher therefore instructed him to pass new orders to the express: its crossing with an eastbound train was to be at Adobe Station, further east than previously scheduled.

RECOMMENDATIONS

The Norwich disaster showed how lax in procedural matters some operators could become. Discipline was emphasized for those employees operating the telegraph.

47

The westbound express continued on, its crew unaware of the altered arrangements, and ran through Adobe without stopping. It met the eastbound train head-on between there and Florence. Two coaches were crushed and burnt out, and 34 people were killed.

Just over a year later, in July 1907, there was a tragedy near Salem, Michigan. The order given to a freight-train crew had been written in a diagonal scrawl, so that the crew thought they were to perform a crossing move at a station further ahead than the one which was intended. The result was a head-on collision when the freight train met a passenger train between the two stations. This time 30 people were killed.

Some three months later, in September 1907 at Canaan in New Hampshire, the wrong train number had been written on a westbound freight train's order. This led its crew to go forward in the belief that they were to pass the scheduled second of two passenger expresses that normally ran 20 minutes apart, because the first train was (they thought) running late and thus behind the second train. The freight train's crew planned, therefore, to go into the sidings at West Canaan, which they could do in ample time to shunt off the main line, as provided for in the standing instructions. However, the first train was in fact running on schedule. It and the freight train collided head-on before the latter reached Canaan. Although a baggage car next to the tender of the express locomotive took much of the impact, the following coach telescoped into it: 26 passengers were killed.

During the 1930s, a new form of signalling control – known as CTC (Centralized Traffic Control) – was being developed for long single-track routes. The signals at crossing loops and sidings were operated by a central despatching office or control centre that could be over 100 miles (160 km) away. CTC had in-built automated safety features and thus had the potential to circumvent the inherent possibilities for human error in the telegraph and train-order system. Even by the 1950s, though, CTC was only just catching on, and more years would pass before it was installed widely. Certainly, by 1950, it had not reached the Canadian National (CN) main line through the Rockies towards Vancouver.

One word, a station name, was missed out of the written train order given to the driver of a westbound extra troop train on 21 November 1950. The result was a massive head-on collision in the mountains with an eastbound passenger train.

The Kamloops despatcher, responsible for this section of the line, had by telephone instructed the telegraph operator at Red Pass to issue an order to the driver of the troop train to cross train No 2 at Cedarside, 35 miles (56 km) on, and train No 4 at

Gosnell, another 25 miles (40 km) away. Although the operator at Red Pass confirmed the message correctly, in writing the order he omitted the vital name 'Cedarside', so that it looked as if the troop train were to pass both trains at Gosnell. The troop train therefore sped through Cedarside and met train No 2 – hauled by a big 4-8-2 locomotive – head-on. Both engine crews died, as did 17 passengers, with many more injured.

Collision at Abermule, Wales, 1921

Once the electric-tablet system – and the later, similar staff and token systems (see page 11) – had been developed, it was gradually adopted on most of the longer single lines in the UK that had to carry several trains on the same route at the same time. The shorter single lines, which might have only one train shuttling backwards and forwards, were a different matter, and so were worked more simply. For 45 years after a telegraph mix-up caused a collision at Radstock, Somerset, in 1876, there were no more head-on collisions involving passenger trains on single lines in the UK (aside from the runaway coaches at Armagh – see page 25). Then came the morning of 26 January 1921.

The Cambrian main line from Whitchurch and Oswestry to Aberystwyth and Pwllheli was single throughout, and was worked by the electric-tablet system. As a hangover from the days of the telegraph, the tablet instruments were sometimes housed in the station office rather than the signalbox, and this was the case at Abermule. The station was also unusual in that the signalbox at its north end did not control the points at the south end, which were worked by a small lever-frame alongside. In those days every single-line section had its own interlocked tablet instruments, one each at the passing stations at the ends of the section. The tablets were round – rather like a thick biscuit – and were notched in such a way that they would fit only into the drawer slides of the instruments to which they should be applied; in other words, a tablet for one section could not be fitted into the instruments in the adjacent sections. Furthermore, the instruments at each end of a single-line section were electromechanically interlocked, so that only one tablet could be drawn from either of them at any one time.

The Abermule disaster was caused by carelessness and a lack of coordination between the four staff at Abermule Station, just like the mix-up at Norwich in 1874 (see page 47). A local train from Whitchurch to Aberystwyth was correctly signalled from Montgomery, next station to the north, to Abermule, and the

Abermule signalman operated the tablet instrument to accept the train. An Aberystwyth–Manchester express was scheduled to pass the local at Abermule but, if either train were late, the crossing place might be changed. That day the express was on time. The relief stationmaster on duty, who should have supervised the passing of the express, was away having his lunch. The signalman went to the signalbox to open the level-crossing gates and 'clear' the signals for the arrival of the local.

A junior porter – who knew how to work the tablet instruments but who should never have touched them – was the only person in the station office when Newtown, next station to the south, asked for the tablet release to send the express from there through to Abermule. The lad gave the release and then went to the levers at the station's southern end, ready to work them for the arrival of the express. A second junior clerk took the tablet – in its leather pouch – from the driver of the local train which had just arrived. He was about to take it to the instrument for the section from Montgomery when the stationmaster saw him, took the pouch from him without looking at it, and, thinking the express had not reached Newtown, gave it back to the local train's driver. He was the last line of defence. He should have read the inscription on the tablet . . . but he didn't, and so he set off for Newtown.

The local train accelerated up the gradient towards Newtown. Some 1³/4 miles (2.4 km) from Abermule the express was running at about 50 mph (80 kmh) downhill, ready to slow for Abermule. Fortunately its driver saw the smoke and steam from the oncoming local and applied full brakes. He managed to slow his speed to about 30 mph (50 kmh), so that the total impact velocity of the two engines was about 60 mph (100 kmh). The express driver and fireman jumped just before the collision and

survived, but the crew of the local engine, the express's guard and 14 passengers were killed.

The express driver found, amid the wreckage of his engine, the tablet he had been carrying. Labelled Newtown–Abermule, it confirmed that his was the only train that should have been in the section. The inquiry afterwards decided the system itself had been at fault: tablet instruments should always be in the signalbox, and signals should be interlocked with tablet instruments so that signals could not be cleared unless the correct tablet had been drawn out.

Collision near Warngau, West Germany, 1975

Sophisticated automated safety equipment has been developed, yet the timetable and train-order system is still employed in parts of the world, even – on some secondary or branch lines – in Europe. This was the case in 1975 on the branch that ran to Lenggries in the Bavarian Alps, near the Austrian border. The line operated according to the timetable, supplemented by telephone between the crossing stations as a form of absolute block. A prescribed form of words was intended to ensure that messages were clearly understood.

On 8 June 1975 traffic into the mountains was heavy, and an extra train was booked from Lenggries to Munich to help bring back weekend holidaymakers and hikers from the mountains. The timetable graph showed a number of what are called conditional train times: if extra trains are needed, they run in the 'conditional' times. On single lines, this might mean a regular train would have to run a few minutes behind schedule to make a safe crossing with an extra. Some of the lines on the timetable graph actually crossed in between stations – an impossible situation – but the intention was that the actual crossing places would be arranged by the local supervisors.

With the extra train from Lenggries running that evening, the regular train from Munich should have waited at Warngau while the extra ran the three miles (5 km) from the next station, Schaftlach. The two supervisors, one each at Warngau and Schaftlach, were busy: they had to issue tickets, operate the telephones and signals and oversee the trains as they arrived and departed. When one called up the other by telephone they each announced their own train was ready to go forward on the single line, and each was under the impression that he had received permission for this to happen. Quite what they said to each other was never really established, but clearly they did not use the prescribed form of words.

Right: The head-on collision at Warngau in Germany in 1975 resulted in massive damage to coaches from an impact speed of 90 mph (145 kmh). It was caused by slack telephone procedures between supervisors at adjacent stations.

RECOMMENDATIONS

Warngau emphasized the necessity for adherence to a precise form of verbal instructions and the need for better staff training. Modern signalling would have prevented the accident.

Left: The Warngau collision was so violent that the diesel locomotives were compressed to about two-thirds of their length. Inevitably, both drivers were killed.

Whatever the case, both trains started off on the single line, heading towards each other. Both were diesel-hauled, but the drivers had little time for their brakes to take effect when they saw each other. The two trains met at a combined speed of over 90 mph (145 kmh). The locomotives were impacted to two-thirds of their length as frames and bodywork buckled; the leading coaches, made of lightweight steel, were compressed and others were thrown over the two locomotives – with roofs, sides and floors bursting open. In all 38 passengers, both drivers and one of the train conductors were killed, while 122 passengers were badly injured . . . all because of slack observance of telephone procedures.

Collision at Cowden, Sussex, 1994

By the 1990s, most lines in the UK had been re-equipped with modern signalling with full track circuiting, colour-light signals and centralized control. Although modern signalling primarily benefits main lines, in some areas local cross-country and branch routes also have modern signalling for operating convenience and added safety. One such line was the Uckfield branch, part of the south of London outer suburban network. The line was not electrified, being operated by diesel-electric multiple units.

Although originally a double-track line, this became single-track in the late 1980s, with a passing loop at Ashurst. The whole line was under the control of Oxted signalling centre, and there was no token system. The drivers were expected to obey the signals, and were helped by the automatic warning system (AWS) fitted to distant and stop signals.

On the morning of 15 October 1994 it was foggy. A train from Oxted to Uckfield had passed 'clear' signals as it left Hever to enter the single-line section. It called at Cowden Station on the single line, and then restarted towards Ashurst. However, an up-train from Uckfield to Oxted, having called at Ashurst, failed to stop at the 'danger' signal about half a mile (800 m) from Ashurst Station, even though, as far as could be ascertained afterwards, the driver had received and acknowledged an audible AWS warning in his cab. The signalling staff at Oxted had a warning that the up-train had irregularly entered the single line but, having no radio communication with the trains, could do nothing to avoid the inevitable head-on collision.

Both trains soon accelerated and, when they met, the impact damage was severe, the leading coach of the up-train being totally destroyed. Both drivers were killed, as was the up-train's guard who, against the rules, was riding with the driver – there were suggestions that he had in fact been driving at the time. Two of the passengers on the up-train also died.

The accident brought to light the risks that could be incurred if signals were not observed and acted on, and raised the question of automatic train protection (ATP) being introduced. This would have given total automated supervision of the actions of both drivers, so that the trains would have been stopped. However, ATP is very expensive – particularly if added to existing signalling – and other methods, not requiring full automation, of reducing the risks of driver error on single and double lines are being examined.

Opposite page: One of the coaches in the Cowden head-on collision hangs precariously over the edge of an embankment. Single line head-on collisions in Britain are rare. In the 118 years from 1876 to 1994 only three serious ones have involved passenger trains, although others have happened at junctions with single tracks.

Left: Despite their sturdy design and build quality, even steel-bodied coaches cannot withstand a high-speed head-on impact.

CHAPTER 6

HIGH-SPEED WRECKS AND RUNAWAYS

For the safe operation of trains, it is essential that drivers keep within the maximum speed limits on curves, through points and switches and over civil-engineering structures like bridges. On downward gradients speed must be controlled, to allow braking in compliance with any lower speed limits ahead. In the nineteenth century, before power brakes that ran right through trains began to be adopted, braking was primitive: there were hand brakes on coaches and wagons, but on any given train only a few of these would be attended by a brakesman. There might also be a steam brake on the locomotive and a hand brake on the tender. Well into this century, freight trains in continental Europe did not always have continuous brakes, and in the UK it was not until the 1970s that the last freight trains relying only on engine brakes and a handbrake in the guard's van at the back finally disappeared. For obvious reasons such trains were always restricted to a fairly conservative maximum speed.

Plunging through open bridges

Left: On 5 June 1975, Locomotive No. 86 242 hauling the overnight Euston–Glasgow sleeping-car train finished up on Nuneaton platform after it derailed. Temporary warning lights, placed along the line had run out of gas, so the driver of the train did not see the speed restriction warnings and approached Nuneaton station too fast.

Where railways cross navigable waterways, either the bridge has to be high enough to allow the tallest ships through or there has to be an opening span. This moveable span might swing on a vertical pivot, be shifted on a hinge at one end or be bodily lifted vertically. Whatever system is used, trains scheduled to cross the bridge must be properly signalled and controlled. There have been a handful of opening bridges on UK main lines, and none has been involved in a disaster. Opening bridges on main lines have been more numerous in coastal and estuary areas in the USA and parts of Europe.

One of the earliest US disasters involving a drawbridge was that which occurred on 6 May 1853 at Norwalk, Connecticut. An express from New York to Boston was approaching South Norwalk Station at speed when its engineer saw the drawbridge ahead was open to shipping. The primitive brakes on the train allowed no hope of stopping in time. The train reached the end of the rails. The locomotive plunged into the water, to be followed by the baggage car and the first two passenger coaches, all initially one on top of the other. The third passenger coach broke up as it went partly over the edge, adding to the heap. The casualties were high – 46 dead – but could have been higher; luckily the passengers on the train included many doctors who were returning from a medical convention, and they were able to give instant help to survivors. The engineer himself lived.

The signal did not give a positive 'danger' indication, consisting simply of a ball that was hauled to the top of a mast for 'clear' (the 'highball') and lowered for 'danger', in which position it was probably invisible. The driver had not been on the line for some time and presumably had forgotten the layout.

Much the same thing happened in October 1906 at Atlantic City, where the Pennsylvania line crossed a river. By this time trains were equipped with fast-acting air brakes and signals had improved vastly since 1853, Even though warning and stop signals showed 'danger', the train swept by with little reduction in speed. Eventually the conductor, realizing what was about to happen, applied the emergency brake. He was too late: the locomotive and two coaches dropped off the bridge into the water below, and 57 passengers died.

Modane, 1917

During wartime troops and *matériel* have to be moved in large quantities by rail to and from active service. This has been especially true in Europe during the two world wars. In war conditions the niceties of established rules and standards of equipment are not always maintained.

Modane Station stands just on the French side of the Mont Cenis Tunnel that runs through the French Alps on the main line from Turin in north-west Italy to Lyon. Northwards from Modane, the line drops sharply down the valley on gradients as steep as 1 in 33; normally in the days of steam there were strict limits on train weights.

On 12 December 1917 French troops returning on leave from fighting in north-eastern Italy were being conveyed in two special trains from Turin. These were coupled together to form a train of 19 coaches, even though there was just one 4-6-0 steam locomotive at the front. Only three coaches next to the locomotive had the automatic air brake; the others had either none at all or only hand brakes controlled by brakesmen. The train was almost four times the weight permitted for the locomotive, and the driver protested. However, the military authorities insisted on starting, threatening him with army discipline.

The inevitable happened as the train started down the steep gradient: the brakes could not hold the heavy load and by the next station, four miles (6 km) down the valley, the train was well out of control with its speed rising above 75 mph (120 kmh). The white hot brake blocks had already started fires as the leading coach derailed and the whole train hurtled into a mounting pile of wreckage which caught fire. There were few survivors and of the 1000 or so troops on board only 425 of the dead could be identified. Estimates put the death toll at around 800 making it the world's worst train accident in terms of casualties, but war conditions were undoubtedly to blame.

Wadenswil, 1948

Wadenswil, on the southern shore of Lake Zurich, is a junction on the Swiss Federal Railways (SBB) main line from Zurich to Chur, in the south-east of the country. It is joined here by a cross-country line of the private South Eastern Railway (SOB) which climbs over the high ground to the south from the Lake of Lucerne region. For a standard-gauge line, the SOB has some fearsome gradients, among the world's steepest not to have rack-and-pinion or cogwheel assistance: several lengths have inclines between 1 in 20 and 1 in 24.

On 22 February 1948 a winter-sports excursion train had run from Zurich over the SOB to the west end of the line; it was due to return just before 17.00. The train was formed of SBB stock, including an articulated electric goods locomotive of the type often known as 'crocodiles'. The train had an SBB driver, accompanied by an SOB pilotman to ensure that he knew the speed limits and the locations of all the signals. The first part of the return journey included steep climbs so the train had an extra electric motor coach at the back to help push it up the hills. But, after Biberbrugg Station, everything was very steeply downhill over the 7 miles (12 km) to Wadenswil. The crocodile had three types of brake: an electric regenerative brake (this works on the principle that the motors become generators and feed current back into the overhead wires, thereby having a braking effect), a non-automatic air brake (used for holding trains on gradients) and the automatic air brake.

At first the train's speed was held within the limits but, just before Samstagern Station, about halfway, the velocity began to rise. As far as the driver was aware, all the brakes had been applied, including the regenerative brake – which alone should have been able to keep the train down to near the 22 mph (35 kmh) speed limit. The pilotman climbed over the balcony at the back end of the locomotive to apply the handbrakes on the first coach in case the air brakes were not working. Despite his efforts, the speed rose towards 40 mph (65 kmh), and the train ran past 'danger' signals at Burghalden, the last station before Wadenswil. At Wadenswil itself, both the tracks allocated to SOB trains were already occupied by loaded passenger trains. Standing instructions were that, in such circumstances, the SOB points on the way into the station should be set towards a siding. The staff at Wadenswil had been told by telephone that a train was out of control no more than two miles (3 km) away, and had no time to do anything other than switch the points. The runaway train sped into the siding, ran through buffers and piled into a new building which collapsed on top of it.

This disaster claimed 21 dead – including the driver and the pilotman – and over 40 injured. Later it was discovered that the driver had mistakenly switched the control wheel used by both the electric brake and the traction supply to the motors to 'power on' instead of 'brake on'. The locomotive was thus under power, accelerating despite the pressure of the brake-blocks. As it was a very powerful goods locomotive, the motors and the gradient won the contest.

Derailment at Sutton Coldfield, near Birmingham, 1955

There was no long drawn-out panic of a runaway train speeding to disaster in the high-speed wreck at Sutton Coldfield on 23 January 1955. Everything was over in less than a minute.

Sutton Coldfield lies on a suburban route between Birmingham and Lichfield High Level (above the Trent Valley line station). Approaching the station from Lichfield is a fairly sharp curve, on which in 1955 the speed limit was 40 mph (65 kmh), followed by a tunnel and then a very sharp left-hand curve through the platforms, where there was a 30 mph (50 kmh) speed restriction. Although this was a local line, it was used also as a diversionary route for trains between Derby and Birmingham on occasions when the main line through Tamworth was blocked by engineering work.

That was the situation on that Sunday. The booked driver of the 12.15 York–Bristol express did not know the line through Sutton Coldfield, so handed over the steam locomotive – a Class 5 4-6-0 – to a conductor-driver who did know it. But,

Left: The breakdown crane lifting gear is attached to the Class 5 4-6-0 locomotive still on its side after overturning when it took the sharp curve at Sutton Coldfield too fast. On the right are the mangled coaches of the derailed train.

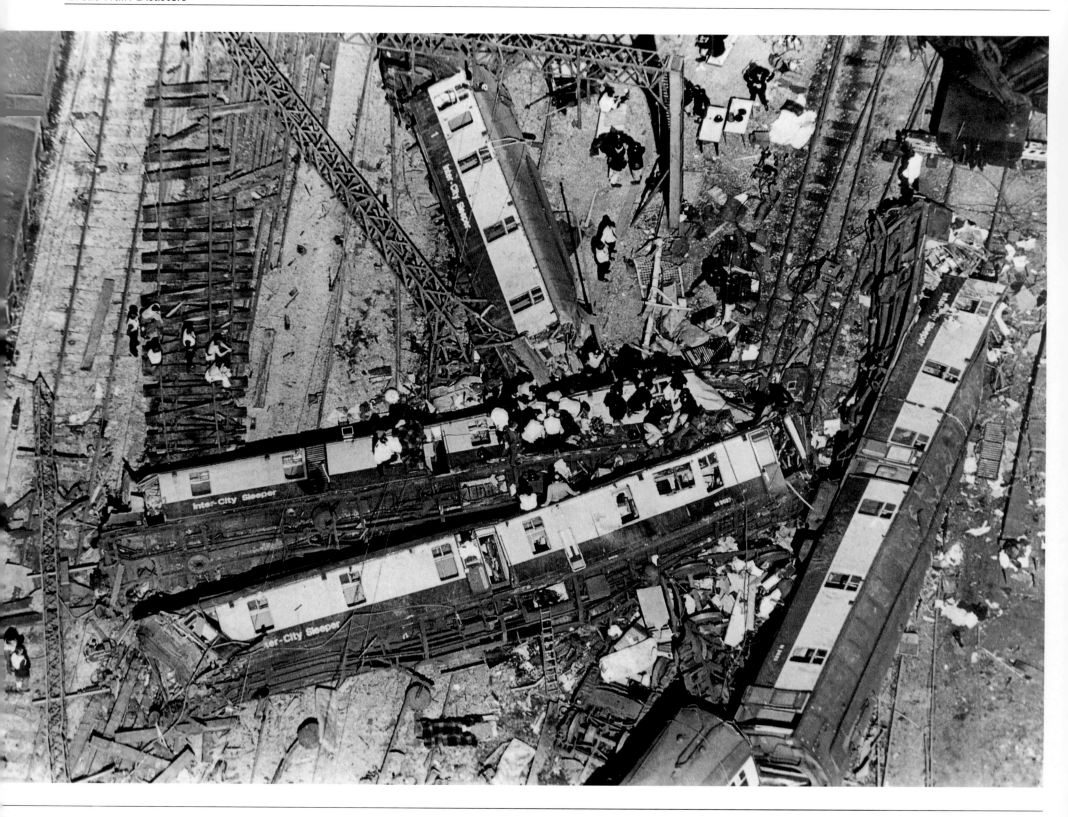

although the conductor driver had driven goods and local passenger trains through Sutton Coldfield, he had not taken many expresses over it. He allowed the speed to rise above the 40 mph (65 kmh) restriction of the right-hand curve, went into the tunnel much faster than he should have done, and was travelling at about 60mph (100 kmh) as the locomotive emerged onto the 30 mph (50 kmh) curve through the station. The engine rolled over onto the opposite platform and the leading coaches spread across both tracks; the other platform and two coaches were destroyed. Of the 300 or so passengers, 14 died, as did three enginemen; 23 passengers were injured. The booked driver survived.

The speed restriction was not marked, only listed in the regulations which the driver was supposed to know by heart. The inquiry into this disaster called for the marking of speed limits, as was already the practice on part of the railway network in eastern England. Even this proved not to be adequate: after a derailment at 80 mph (130 kmh) on the 40 mph (65 kmh) curve at Morpeth on the main East Coast route between London and Scotland in May 1969, selected speed limits in the UK were given more advanced warnings and AWS equipment. After another derailment at Morpeth in 1984 – this time with the train going in the opposite direction – on a stretch of track which surprisingly had not been considered to require improved marking and AWS, despite the earlier accident, the advanced warnings and AWS were applied more widely. Today nearly all permanent speed restrictions are marked, even if not accompanied by AWS.

Derailments at Nuneaton, 1975, and Argenton sur Creuse, 1985

Temporary speed restrictions – because of engineering work on the track or on bridges and other structures – have nearly always been marked by lineside signs showing both speed limits and the points between which they applied. Usually there is (a) an advance-warning sign at the place where the train must begin to slow down, (b) another sign where the speed restriction starts, by which time the speed of the train must be no higher than the limit, and (c) another marking the place where the train can once again accelerate to normal speed. These signs must be visible at night. In the UK they were initially illuminated internally by oil lamps. More recently they have been illuminated by bottled gas lamps or floodlit externally.

During 1975 the tracks through Nuneaton Station were being rebuilt. A 20 mph (32 kmh) speed restriction had been applied over the remaining lines, some of which had short tight curves where old lines joined new ones. About a mile (1.6 km) from the station, on the main line from London Euston, was the advance-warning board: it was illuminated by gas lamps to show two horizontal yellow lights, and, silhouetted, the speed limit in figures. But on the night of 5 June the bottled gas was running out, and the reserve bottle had not been correctly linked. Several trains passed late that night as the lights got dimmer. Eventually they went out altogether. Then the 23.30 Euston–Glasgow sleeper train, which was running late and whose driver was trying to make up time, approached. The driver looked for the lights but could not see them. Too late, he realized he must have missed the warning. When he saw the start-of-restriction board near the station he was still travelling at about 80 mph (130 kmh).

The electric locomotive derailed and rode up onto the platform, damaging the canopy, and the leading coaches were spreadeagled across the tracks. Astonishingly, only six people died, with 38 injured. Part of the blame was put on the driver, but others – including the drivers of earlier trains, who had not reported the dimming lights, and the track staff, who had not connected the bottled gas properly – shared the guilt.

The accident highlighted inconsistent procedures. As a result, improved warning-board designs were introduced, as was AWS track equipment that gave an audible warning in the cab that there was a speed-restriction area ahead.

A decade later at Argenton, on the French main line between Paris and Toulouse, another driver became confused when encountering a temporary speed restriction. He observed the warning but failed to slow down, assuming the start-of-restriction board was a second advance warning. In fact he should have reduced speed to 20 mph (32 kmh) at that point but he failed to do so. The train was derailed. Worse came. A train travelling in the opposite direction ploughed into the wreckage, and 43 people were killed.

Collision at Paris Gare de Lyon, 1988

One of the worst runaway disasters of recent years was that at Paris Gare de Lyon on 27 June 1988. This station has two principal parts: there is the main-line station at ground level and a suburban station underground, beneath the main platforms. Trains run into and out of the

Opposite page: An aerial view of the derailed sleeping cars scattered across Nuneaton station in June 1975. Six passengers and staff died in the accident.

Right: The badly deformed and crushed coaches at Paris Gare de Lyon after a runaway suburban electric train travelling steeply downhill rammed a similar train waiting to leave the terminus in June 1988.

four-track dead-end suburban station on steeply graded lines that link with the main-line junctions on the surface.

A suburban electric train from Melun had been delayed for nearly half an hour because a passenger had pulled the alarm signal. The driver and conductor could not find anything wrong, and so tried to reset the alarm in order that the brakes would be released. The driver, still with problems, operated an isolating valve, not realizing that he had just turned off the brakes on most of his train. As the train started to drop down the steep (1 in 25) gradient towards the underground terminus, speed rose rapidly. For some reason the driver did not apply the electric brake but instead relied on the automatic air brake, which was not being applied right through the train. The driver

called up the station inspector by radio to tell him that he could not stop; after passing 'danger' signals approaching the station, his train collided head-on with another of the same type standing in the platform and already packed with homeward-bound commuters waiting to leave. The heavy motor coach sliced into the lighter front coach of the waiting train, cutting it more or less in two. Both trains were crowded. 59 people, including the driver of the waiting train – who was trying to get passengers out – were killed and 32 were injured.

The disaster brought pressure for adoption of more automation and speed supervision in ATP. Isolating valves were removed, so that no longer could brakes be turned off between coaches of suburban trains.

The runaway near Piacenza, 1997

For the last 25 years engineers have been developing trains with tilting bodies designed to take curves on existing lines (built over the last century) faster than conventional trains. The bodies tilt or lean into the curve like a motorcyclist around a bend, enabling passengers to sit comfortably because they are not thrown sideways as they would be on a conventional train at the same speed. In the early 1980s British Rail tried the tilting Advanced Passenger Train, but it was not reliable. Today, the Italian and Swedish train builders have tilting trains in service.

The Italian tilting Pendolino trains are being introduced on several lines in Italy and Switzerland, including the Milan-Rome route, and can take curves about 12–15 mph (20–25 kmh) faster than other trains. But on 12 January 1997 a Pendolino train took the curve at Piacenza with its 62 mph (105 kmh) speed restriction at about 100 mph (160 kmh). Eight of the nine coaches were derailed, most tipping on to their sides. The leading coach hit one of the masts supporting the overhead conductor wires and was ripped open from end to end killing eight people and injuring 29. Six of the dead were railway staff, two of whom were the drivers of the train. Automatic train protection (ATP) supervising train speed is not generally fitted on existing lines in Italy, but the Piacenza curve was provided with an ATP speed limit beacon. Initial investigations suggested that the beacon speed control was set at too high a level and did not exercise control over a train taking the curve too fast. No train, even with a tilting capability, could hold the track at such excess speeds.

OUTCOME

The Piacenza accident was a result of excessive speed and, possibly, a wrongly calibrated speed limit beacon. Proposals to prevent a recurrence had not been made at the time of writing.

Left: The remains of the tilting Pendolino train which took the curve at Piacenza much too fast and overturned. One coach was ripped open and eight people died.

CHAPTER 7

EQUIPMENT FAILURES

One of the worst structural failures that can beset a railway is a bridge collapse – especially if the bridge falls down when a train happens to be on it. Floods and raging torrents after heavy rainstorms can have a devastating effect, although the elements may not always be entirely to blame.

In May 1847 a train from Chester to Ruabon was crossing the bridge over the River Dee when the driver felt the bridge moving. He accelerated and, just as the engine reached the other side, the bridge fell into the river, taking the tender and the coaches with it and killing five people, four of them railwaymen. The bridge, designed by Robert Stephenson, had girders made of cast-iron. Examination of the broken girder afterwards proved the danger of cast-iron: the material was brittle and had no strength in tension. Engineers everywhere were accordingly warned off cast-iron for bridge girders. Robert Stephenson himself suffered both an inquiry and an inquest, but was exonerated. Wrought-iron was found to be much stronger, and was used for many bridges until the advent of steel, later in the century.

An almost identical accident to the Dee bridge disaster happened in 1876 at Ashtabula Creek, Ohio, though with far more serious consequences. The Pacific express, heading west from New York, was being hauled by two locomotives. As it crossed the bridge over the creek, 75 ft (23 m) above the stream, the engineer of the lead locomotive felt the bridge move and despairingly applied more steam. His engine just made land as the bridge collapsed behind. The coupling to the second engine broke, and that engine and the entire seven-car train fell, with the bridge, into a mound of wreckage. The wooden-bodied cars were lit by oil lamps and heated by coal-burning stoves, and within minutes the unfortunate train had caught fire. It is not known how many passengers were on the train, but only 52 were brought out alive. The death toll was officially stated as 83, but there may have been many more unaccounted for in the fire. The bridge was of trussed-iron construction and, when it had been built 13 years earlier, some engineers had criticized its design. Whatever faults there might have been in the bridge, the disaster led to legislation in 1887 for a formal system for reporting and investigating fatalities in US train accidents, so that safety recommendations could be laid down for the future.

A second train ran past the 'clear' signal and ploughed into the back of the first one. Within a few seconds a third, fortunately empty, train, coming the other way, collided with the wreckage.

Left: The Clapham Junction disaster in 1988. When one train ran into the back of another because of a wrong signal indication, some coaches were thrown into the path of an empty train and 35 passengers died.

Right: The broken iron spans of the Dee bridge at Chester, after they had collapsed and thrown a train into the river.

Undoubtedly the worst bridge disaster in the UK was that on the Tay Bridge, which collapsed in 1879. The bridge was 2¾ miles (3.6 km) long: the longest railway bridge in the country (and indeed at the time in the world), it spanned a tidal estuary. It thus had all the forces of moving water around the foundations and supports while also being open to wind and weather. From the start of its construction there had been problems: the engineers had assumed there would be plenty of rock beneath the water on which they could build the foundations, but there proved to be very little. Instead they managed with the largely soft material of the river bed, instead building the bridge off masonry bases – six vertical cast-iron columns being constructed for each pier. The columns, filled with concrete, were in sections, bolted together; as many as seven sections on top of each other were needed to reach the height of the track. They were braced by wrought-iron tie-bars, attached to lugs. On the piers were carried the main trussed wrought-iron girders that supported the single line of railway. Even at the formal inspection for approval to open the bridge, in 1878, there were one or two misgivings concerning the effect strong winds might have. After a few months, tie-bars were discovered to have worked loose, and their fastenings were thereafter constantly tightened. Also, some of the lugs on the cast-iron columns were found to be defective because of poor casting.

The evening of Sunday 28 December 1879 was wet and stormy, with severe gales. The afternoon train for Dundee waiting at Burntisland for the passengers being ferried across the Forth estuary from Edinburgh must have represented a haven for the people who had endured such a rough crossing. The gale was blowing really hard as the train then moved onto the Tay Bridge's single track.

The train was partway across when observers on shore saw sparks and flame falling into the river. But not just sparks were involved: towards the centre of the bridge the line passed through its structural girders, and the whole of this 13-span high-girder section, with the train inside it, was blown into the river. Not a single person on board survived; although the number of passengers was not known exactly, since their tickets had been collected at a previous station, a careful check suggested that 80 people died, including the train crew. The engine was later lifted from the mud on the river bed and put back into working order.

Examination afterwards by a committee of engineers, as part of a full court of inquiry, found that the bridge was badly designed, badly built and badly maintained. A new bridge was opened in 1887, and survives to this day. The fall of the first bridge gave a sharp reminder that the effect of wind strengths had to be calculated in bridge designs and strong materials should be used in their construction, with wrought-iron or preferably steel instead of cast-iron.

Before the century was out another major bridge collapse occurred as a consequence of inadequate constructional strength. This time it was in the country where bridge builders were regarded as the best in the world at the art of taking railways through impossible terrain: Switzerland. But at Munchenstein, just outside Basel, on the afternoon of Sunday, 14 June 1891 it was Ashtabula Creek (see page 63) all over again. The bridge over the River Birs had been designed and built by Gustave Eiffel (1832–1923), of Eiffel Tower fame, and completed in 1875. It was of unusual design for an iron bridge, with triangular framework forming the main structure. One of the piers had been damaged during floods in 1881, but the structure had been repaired and nine years later some of the supporting structure had been strengthened to take heavier trains – although this did not include the main 138 ft (42 m) span.

That Sunday a heavy train of 13 coaches, hauled by two locomotives, was on its way from Basel to Delemont when it reached the Birs Bridge. At first the engine crews felt the locomotives roll to the right in a twisting movement, and then they were hurtling down the 30 ft (10 m) or so into the river as the span collapsed from the centre. The two locomotives and the leading seven coaches finished up as a heap of wreckage amid the torn and twisted iron of the bridge. One coach hung perilously on the edge of the abutment at the Basel end. Five coaches remained on the track. Even though the drop into the water was nothing like as great as that at Ashtabula Creek or into the Tay, 71 people died, including the driver of the leading engine; 171 people were injured. As with the Tay Bridge disaster 12 years before, examination of the Birs Bridge found that its design was not strong enough for the loads it was supposed to carry: the iron components were too weak, and there were defects in the bridge's construction.

The Birs Bridge disaster affected railway engineering throughout Europe and undoubtedly brought home the lessons that had to be learnt.

Contich, Belgium, 1908, and Buttevant, Ireland, 1980

These two disasters, although separated by 72 years, arose from precisely the same causes. Once interlocking between signal and points levers had been developed it was adopted gradually in many countries. In the UK, which then included all of Ireland, it became mandatory for passenger lines under the Regulation of Railways Act (1889). Eire has inherited the relevant regulatory procedures and requirements from the days when it was part of the UK.

In 1908 Contich Station, on the Antwerp–Brussels main line, had an interlocking lever frame. But during May of that year repair work was being done, with renewals being carried out to the lever frame. Levers were, one by one, disconnected from the wires to signals and points. Whenever a lever was disconnected, men outside under the direction of the signalman pulled wires by hand, where possible, or lifted balance weights and moved points manually by bars, clamping the switches to the rail alongside.

On the morning of 21 May, work was being done on the lever controlling the entry signal to Contich Station. A loop track led to the platform clear of the main line. Although the points were normally worked from the signalbox, the signal was being worked by hand. A local train had arrived at the platform, and in a matter of minutes an express from Antwerp to Brussels was due. The signalman told the man outside to clear the signal for the express, but forgot that the points lever was still set towards the loop. The express driver suddenly found his train switched to the platform track where it collided with the back of the standing train. As a result, 40 passengers died and over 100 were injured, largely because the express engine destroyed the wooden-bodied coaches of the local train.

On 1 August 1980, at Buttevant in Eire, only one train was involved, but the circumstances were the same as at Contich: levers in the signalbox had been disconnected while work was carried out, so that the security of the interlocking was lost. Buttevant is on the main Dublin–Cork line. Although the station had been closed some years before, there was still a signalbox controlling a level-crossing, a crossover between the main tracks and points into sidings for use by ballast trains.

Earlier in the year the track layout at Buttevant had been changed, with new points replacing old. The signalbox work had not been completed. The points into the siding were now facing to trains from Dublin to Cork but had not been connected to a lever. The new point switches should have been clamped and padlocked as out of use, as required by the rules. However, the rules did allow them to be used under clearly prescribed circumstances: in such instances, if the main line was open to traffic, the protecting signals had to be disconnected and kept at 'danger', with any train passing doing so at very low speeds and signalled by flags.

But the rules were not being followed that day, and indeed hadn't been for some weeks. The siding points were being used by ballast trains, and the switches were being moved by a man

Opposite: Searching for survivors in vain, after the collapse of the Tay Bridge in 1879 during high winds. The whole centre section, including the train which was trapped within the girder structure, was blown into the river with not a single survivor.

with a crowbar on instructions from the signalman. The normal signals were being worked from the signalbox, free of interlocking with the relevant points. The pointsman saw a locomotive arrive from Mallow, to the south, and assumed it was the next train to be diverted into the sidings, so he set the points accordingly. But the signalman, not seeing the pointsman's action, cleared all the signals for the 10.00 express from Dublin to Cork. The trap was set. The express approached at speed and, although just at the last moment the signalman realized what the pointsman had done and put the signals for the express back to 'danger', the express rocketed into the siding and piled up behind the diesel locomotive. The timber-bodied coaches at the front were reduced to matchwood. In all, 18 people were killed – including two members of the train crew – and 75 were injured.

Although the accident was directly caused by the pointsman's erroneous assumption, it brought to light a total disregard of procedures at all levels and in all the engineering departments concerned with the line.

Derailment at Bihta, India, 1937

The derailment at about 60 mph (100 kmh) of the overnight express from the Punjab to Calcutta on straight track killed over 100 passengers. It resulted in a number of official inquiries, since there were political implications for the Indian Government and not least for the UK's involvement in India. A committee of eminent engineers from the UK, France and India, under the chairmanship of the UK Chief Inspecting Officer of Railways, found the design of the Pacific-type locomotive was at fault: it swayed from side to side because of improper spring-control on the front and back wheels, and this damaged the track, particularly where the ground under the track-bed was soft and even more particularly when it had been affected by heavy rain in monsoon periods. There had been, the inquiry decided, other derailments and many instances of track distortion because of this.

Derailment at Frankford Junction, Philadelphia, 1943

The danger of overheated axle-bearings was amply demonstrated by the derailment of a Washington–New York express at Frankford Junction in September 1943. Right from the early days of railways, the ends of the axles were carried in axle-boxes with plain – usually white-metal – bearings, lubricated originally by grease and later by oil through impregnated pads. If the axle-box was not regularly lubricated, the bearing ran dry and overheated. For many years a regular feature of the railways was the wheeltapper. At each station a wheeltapper would walk along the train, tapping the wheels to make sure they gave a resilient ring – which meant they were not cracked – and putting his hand on the axle-box covers to see if they were warming up. A hot axle-box could easily start a fire: wooden coach or wagon bodies could go up in flames, or the steel axle could become red-hot to the stage where the metal weakened and sheared off, leaving the wheels without support from the axle-box making derailment inevitable.

The Frankford Junction derailment was one of the worst to arise from this cause. An axle running in plain bearings under a dining car became so hot that its end broke off, and a derailment ensued. Unfortunately the coach tilted sideways to hit a signal gantry, which cut right through it. There were heavy casualties: 79 dead and 103 injured.

The cure for such eventualities was the use of roller bearings. These were in fact already being fitted to many US coaches, and in the past 50 years they have become widespread on passenger and freight rolling stock around the world. However, even roller bearings with long-life lubrication need maintenance, and even today axle-box failures are not unknown. Nowadays there is lineside equipment which can detect hot axle-boxes and give warnings to the control centre or by radio to the locomotive crew.

Collision at Lichfield, Staffordshire, 1946

In any interlocking system, signals and points have to agree. At least, that is what everyone thought until New Year's Day 1946. We have already seen what happened when signals and points disagreed in the Tamworth disaster of 1870 (see page 22). The next station to the north, Lichfield Trent Valley, had much the same layout, with platform loop tracks diverging from what was otherwise a double-track main line. By 1946, however, full interlocking had been provided at Lichfield for about 70 years.

A southbound local passenger train from Stafford to Rugby was signalled into the platform loop, where it was to wait while an express freight train, carrying fish from Fleetwood to London Broad Street, passed by. The Lichfield signalman cleared the passenger train from the block instruments from Armitage, the next signalbox to the north, and accepted the fish train, immediately asking permission to send it southward. He unlocked the set of points over which the passenger train had passed to reach the platform line, then operated the lever to set the points for the main line. He relocked them and cleared the signals for the fish train to run through on the centre track.

The fish train, approaching at over 40 mph (65 kmh) suddenly swung over the points towards the loop track. It ploughed through most of the four coaches of the local train.

killing 20 passengers and injuring most of the others. Investigations afterwards showed that, on this bitterly cold evening, frozen stone ballast had prevented the facing-point lock and its fouling bar from moving when the signalman operated the locking lever: he moved the points lever but the points did not change; instead, the rodding (i.e. the rods to the points) bent as if the points movement had been successful. This meant that the points and lock levers were in position to release the interlocking for the through-line signals. The disaster was one of the very rare cases in the UK of mechanical interlocking failing to prevent an accident.

Below: Wreckage of the four coaches of the local train from Stafford litter the platform at Lichfield after an express fish train had run into them when points had frozen in the wrong position.

Above: Rescuers search an overturned coach after the Hither Green derailment in 1967 caused by a broken rail.

expansion of the rails when the weather was hot. Cracks could, however, develop from the holes; if these were not spotted early on they might enlarge until lumps of steel rail broke away – with potentially lethal consequences. In the past 50 years rail ends have been welded together to reduce this danger.

At Hither Green, in the south-eastern suburbs of London, an accident on the evening of 5 November 1967 showed how devastating the results of a broken rail could be. A piece of rail, 5½ in (14 cm) long, broke away as a crowded 12-coach diesel-electric train from Hastings to London Charing Cross passed over, and the front wheels of the third coach were derailed. These wheels ran derailed for a further ¼ mile (400 m) or so until they hit crossings from another track. This encounter caused most of the rest of the train to derail, so that only the front coach was left on the track. Four coaches overturned, sliding on their sides; it was in these that most of the casualties occurred. All told, 49 passengers were killed and nearly 80 were injured.

Investigations afterwards showed that track maintenance had been poor. Where the break had occurred, short lengths of in-fill rail had been used to link longer lengths, some on wooden sleepers and some on concrete, and so the rails had been subject to uneven stresses. The remedy was a better-quality and better-maintained track.

Tunnel collapse at Vierzy, France, 1972

Vierzy is about 60 miles (100 km) north-east of Paris on the line from Paris Gare du Nord to Hirson, and represents the junction with the line that runs south from Lille to Basel. One of the most remarkable disasters to be caused by an obstruction on the line occurred there on 17 June 1972, when part of the lining of Vierzy tunnel collapsed on to the track. The rubble was not detected and it did not interrupt the signalling. By a cruel trick of fate two trains, both diesel-hauled, entered opposite ends of the tunnel more or less at the same time. They hit the debris, which was invisible from the tunnel's entrances, derailed and became a tightly wedged pile of wreckage. There was nowhere for the kinetic energy of the impact to be dispersed other than through the coaches, which were held in place by the tunnel walls. The result was one of the worst peacetime railway disasters in France: 108 people were killed and no fewer than 240 were injured.

Derailment at Hither Green, London, 1967

When rails were made of iron, breaks were relatively frequent, so that daily track inspection was required. Steel rails were much stronger, but the bolt-holes near the rail ends, where fishplates joined one rail to the next with bolts and nuts were prone to weakness. The idea was that the joints were held together while at the same time there was freedom enough in the connection to allow for the

Derailment and bridge collapse at Sydney, 1977

Echoes of the St Johns disaster (see page 32) were raised by an accident in the suburbs of Sydney, Australia, in January 1977. A local train was travelling at no great speed over poorly maintained track when some of the coaches were derailed. In another location this might have caused little more than a shake-up for the passengers. But, as luck would have it, at the spot where the derailment occurred there was a road overbridge. The derailed coaches struck and displaced supporting piers. The road collapsed on to the tops of the coaches, compressing two of them to a fraction of their original height. 83 passengers were killed and over 200 were injured. This was a tragic demonstration of how lax track-maintenance standards can cause major disasters.

Left: An aerial view of the road overbridge in Sydney which collapsed onto a train below after derailed coaches had dislodged supporting piers. 83 passengers were killed.

OUTCOME

The Clapham accident resulted in an examination of the way major resignalling works were carried out. Methods of management, planning and execution were completely overhauled.

Right: A general view of the Clapham Junction disaster, with the two trains in the first collision on the extreme right and the third train, with its front coaches derailed, on the left.

The Clapham Junction collision, London, 1988

The signal-engineering profession has always had the highest standards. You do not need all the fingers of one hand to count the number of disasters caused in the UK over the past 60 years by technical mistakes on the part of signal engineers. But on the morning of 12 December 1988 at Clapham Junction, the UK's busiest station, carnage was caused when a single wire in a relay room made a false contact with a relay terminal, so making a signal show 'clear' when there was a train on the line ahead of it. A second train ran past the 'clear' signal and ploughed into the back of this first one. Within a few seconds a third, fortunately empty, train coming the other way collided with the wreckage. A single mistake by a signal technician when he had been altering wiring, so that one live wire was left loose and able to touch other equipment, thus bypassing safety relays, cost 35 passengers their lives and injured nearly 70 others.

The accident was so serious that a full judicial inquiry was ordered. The inquiry revealed a whole catalogue of problems involved if major signal-renewal schemes had to be carried out while trains were still operating: there was a shortage of qualified staff (many people were having to work weeks on end with hardly a day off) and poor organization led to a lack of thorough testing and a general decline in standards. There were widespread suggestions in the media that the root cause of the disaster was governmental underfunding of British Rail. Certainly, British Rail was having to work within ever tighter budgets while, battling against an ever larger backlog of renewals as older equipment was wearing out more quickly than it could be replaced.

Some railway accidents have brought new developments or better standards in railway safety in their wake, and the Clapham Junction disaster was one. In its aftermath there had to be a complete rethink concerning how resignalling schemes should be organized and carried out – emphasis was given to improved training schemes for both management and maintenance staff.

Left: Rescuers in the Clapham accident had immense difficulties in getting to survivors trapped among the twisted steel coach bodies, displaced seats and partitions.

CHAPTER 8

FIRE, FLOOD AND SNOW

While one can talk about how rail disasters have been the result of human or technical errors, some have been caused by those elements which humankind has recognized since prehistory as part friend, part foe. Fire warms and water quenches, but both can kill.

Train fires

If a train catches fire when it is on the move, a truly horrific disaster can result. Steps must be taken to extinguish any fire as soon as it is discovered, for a small initial blaze, whipped up by the wind of the train's movement, can soon become a raging conflagration. We have already seen how lighting, from either oil lamps or gas, could conspire with burning coal from locomotive fireboxes to turn the wreckage caused by derailments or collisions into what was, in effect, a funeral pyre. A fire in a tunnel is even worse: toxic fumes quickly build up, so that passengers not killed by the fire itself may die from inhaling poisonous gases.

Two trains passed into an area heavily contaminated with natural gas that had escaped from a broken pipeline. Just one spark or open flame was enough. Both trains were blown to destruction.

On the Paris Metro in August 1903 a seemingly innocuous fire in the driver's power controller (the cause was an electrical fault) produced a major disaster. Electric trains, with motors on some of the coaches – i.e. they were not hauled by a separate locomotive – had recently been developed, and these were what the Metro was using. At first cables ran through the train and worked at the full line voltage. There was considerable risk if there was a short circuit.

Passengers were asked to leave this particular Metro train, the plan being that it be pushed forward by another emptied train to the end of the line. But it had not gone far when the fire broke out in earnest, engulfing the coach in which it had started and sending smoke and fumes along the tunnel. A following train, already overloaded with people unloaded from emptied trains, was evacuated hurriedly but, when the lights went out

and smoke rushed through the tunnel, its passengers panicked and stampeded for the surface. Meanwhile, other people, unaware of what was going on, were trying to get down to the platforms. . . Over 80 people died, from one cause or another.

At London King's Cross Underground Station on 18 November 1987 no train was involved in the fire disaster. A small fire on an escalator up from the deep-level Piccadilly line developed over 15 minutes until there was a sudden flashover. A fireball swept up the escalator tunnel to the booking hall and concourse. Four London Underground lines meet at King's Cross, each having two platforms, and there are various escalators and stairways to the street and to two main-line stations (the other being St Pancras). There were so many ways

Left: Weary firemen pause for fresh air at King's Cross station entrance after the traumatic work of rescue. A small fire on an underground escalator suddenly erupted into a fireball and engulfed 31 passengers.

Right: Little hope of finding survivors in the wreckage of the trains engulfed by exploding natural gas which had leaked over a wide area from a pipeline near Ufa on the Trans-Siberian Railway in 1989. Negligence in not detecting the gas leak was blamed.

Right: The burnt-out ticket hall at the top of the escalator at King's Cross after the devastating fire had been put out.

passengers could get in and out of King's Cross. For a while, Underground trains were still arriving every minute or so. The staff and the handful of police who happened to be on the scene rapidly found the task of evacuation almost impossible. Fire and rescue services soon arrived, but even so 31 people died. King's Cross and adjacent Underground stations stank of burning for weeks afterwards.

The disaster warranted a judicial inquiry, which concluded that it probably started when someone dropped a cigarette end through the escalator steps. The glowing tip ignited grease-impregnated dirt and dust, and the fire then spread to the timber parts of the escalator. The inquiry made over 150 safety recommendations, and as a result there was a complete rethink on fire safety by London Underground. Smoking is now banned anywhere within the system.

A decade earlier on 6 July 1978, at Taunton on the Penzance–Paddington main line, one of the worst tragedies involving fire as the primary cause occurred when flames engulfed a sleeping-car. The coach concerned had a steel body, but the results were no less drastic than they might have been on one of the older wooden coaches because of the amount of flammable material it contained. The fire started because a bag of dirty bed-linen had been left against the outlet of an electric convector heater. This started to smoulder as the train left Exeter, the station down-line from Taunton. Smoke and fumes penetrated the sleeping compartments – partly through the pressure ventilation – and soon the coach was alight. The disaster, which claimed 12 lives, was made worse because the coach's external doors were locked, so that passengers could not escape quickly. The accident highlighted a lack of proper staff training and an absence of fire-safety equipment and procedures.

But on 4 June 1989 at Ufa, on the Trans-Siberian Railway, in the then Soviet Union no amount of railway fire precautions could have prevented the conflagration, which exploded into a fireball over a mile (1.6 km) across. Two trains passed into an area heavily contaminated with natural gas that had escaped from a broken pipeline. Just one spark or open flame – who can tell which? – was enough. Both trains were largely blown to destruction. The death toll has never been properly ascertained, but certainly it ran into hundreds. Of the few survivors, most suffered severe burns.

Fire disasters need not involve the burning of a train. One ghastly event occurred during the Second World War; as with the disaster near Modane in the First World War (see page 56), this was not a direct result of military action but arose from wartime conditions. The southern part of Italy was already in Allied hands by the spring of 1944, but there was still no semblance of civilian normality. Trains were running, with freight trains taking priority. Eastwards from Naples and the Sorrento coastal plain lines ran across the southern Apennines to the Gulf of Taranto, in the heel of Italy. Gradients were steep. On 2 March a heavy freight train, hauled by two 2-8-0 steam locomotives, was running over the line to Potenza. Its load should have been purely goods traffic, but 600 passengers had scrambled on as well – so adding yet further to the weight.

All was not well on the engines, for the coal was poor, containing a great deal of dust; for the same reason it created plenty of thick smoke as it burned. The train started off on the single line from Balvano. As it entered the Armi Tunnel, steam pressure was dropping and the wheels were slipping. Eventually it came to a stop in the middle of the by now smoke-filled tunnel. The train should ideally have backed out, but all too soon carbon-monoxide fumes spread throughout the tunnel and overtook all those inside it; only a few people at the back of the train, still in the open, escaped. Over 400 victims of smoke inhalation and carbon-monoxide poisoning were counted.

Flood and other bridge disasters

Among all the disasters caused by structures failing, more have been as a consequence of the elements than for any other reason. On occasion, as we have seen, the structures themselves may have been badly designed or built, or have been frail because of the construction materials then in use, but over the years, particularly in areas where heavy, prolonged rain is a feature of the weather or in mountainous regions where freak storms can send a concentrated cascade of water down a narrow valley, floods have caused many bridge washouts, sometimes with little warning. Trains have fallen through the gap left by demolished girders or been swept into the water as spans have collapsed beneath them.

The railways of the Indian subcontinent are particularly susceptible to flood damage. Monsoon rains turn rivers into raging torrents that scour even the best of bridge foundations away. Examples of Indian bridges being washed out with no warning to disastrous effect are the tragedy at Mangapatnan in

1902, when the Madras–Bombay mail train was swept away with the loss of over 60 lives, and that near Quilon in 1988, when a Bangalore–Trivandrum express fell into a lake and at least 100 passengers (probably many more) died.

Bridge washouts in other countries tend to be comparatively rare events. In western France, in 1911, a bridge pier collapsed under a train at Montreuil-Bellay, killing 22. Three years later, on the Highland main line in Scotland, a flash flood was caused by a heavy thunderstorm. The flood waters rushed down from the mountains through a narrow gorge, and took out the foundations of a masonry bridge over Baddengorm Burn near Carr Bridge, throwing part of a train into the stream. One coach was battered to matchwood and swept away; five passengers died. Much more recently, on the Llanelli–Craven Arms Central Wales line in October 1987, a two-coach diesel train plunged into the waters of the River Towy while running slowly so that the crew could examine the line. In the darkness the men did not see that Glanrhyd Bridge had collapsed into the swollen river, which had damaged its foundations. Four of the people on the train drowned.

Left: Engineers raise the deck of the bridge which collapsed at Montreuil-Bellay in France in 1911. It had fallen into the river after a pier was demolished, taking a train with it. The locomotive can just be seen at the bottom of the picture.

Right: The badly damaged coaches from the train which plunged into the river at Walouru, New Zealand, on Christmas Eve, 1953. After a volcanic eruption in the mountains, water swept down the river and demolished the railway viaduct.

Right: The badly damaged coaches from the train which plunged into the river at Walouru, New Zealand, on Christmas Eve, 1953. After a volcanic eruption in the mountains, water swept down the river and demolished the railway viaduct.

Right: Snow was the initial cause of the Abbots Ripton accident in 1876 when signals became frozen in the clear position. But the accident brought a change in operating procedures.

Seismic activity, too, has also caused railway disasters – for example the earthquake which struck Japan's island of Honshu in 1923, and caused widespread destruction and death. In New Zealand on Christmas Eve, 1953, a volcanic eruption breached a lake, whose waters cascaded down a river valley. The tidal wave of lake water, ash and ice debris, swept all before it. The bridge over the river at Walouru was washed away and, unseen in the darkness, a train fell from the track into the torrent. Over 150 people lost their lives.

Not all bridge disasters are caused by the elements or structural faults. From time to time railways, despite all safety precautions, are at the mercy of other people's mistakes. Bridge strikes are one example: over-high lorries or other vehicles can jam under rail overbridges and dislodge track. One of the worst disasters caused by outside human error was a river bridge collapse at Mobile, Alabama, in September 1993. A river barge under tow hit a bridge pier. This was not reported and, when a train crossed the bridge a little while later, it collapsed. Part of the train sank into the river, and 47 passengers and crew members died.

Sometimes embankments approaching bridges can be washed away or banks running alongside rivers can be undermined, so

leading to derailments as tracks slip away from under a train. This type of accident has happened in many places. One of the most tragic was in Holland, in September 1918, just before the end of the First World War. Heavy rain made an embankment

that led to a canal bridge near Weesp unstable. The track-bed slipped, tipping a train down the bank so that over 40 passengers were killed.

Disasters in snow

Certainly avalanches in mountainous areas have played their part in various rail accidents, although they have caused few disasters: normally their havoc concerns merely damage to track and disruption to services. But snow can present other threats, particularly the 'wrong' type of snow in the wrong place. A snowstorm was instrumental in causing a major disaster at Abbots Ripton, in England, on 21 January 1876 and played some part in the disaster at Castlecary – in Scotland between Edinburgh and Glasgow – on 10 December 1937.

In the Abbots Ripton tragedy the drama started at Holme when a coal train, running south from Peterborough in a heavy snowstorm, should have been shunted out of the way to let the following Flying Scotsman express go by. The snow was formed of large flakes that quickly clung and built up, in contrast to the fine, dry powdery snow that can blow into the motors of today's electric trains and stop them from working. However, the coal train did not stop, even though the signalbox levers were standing at 'danger'. At the next stop which had a siding, Abbots Ripton, the semaphore signals showed 'clear' for the coal train but the signalman showed the driver a red hand-light, stopping it so that it could be shunted back into the siding. But, as it was in the process of doing so, the Flying Scotsman suddenly emerged at speed out of the darkness and blizzard and ploughed into the back of it. As if that were not enough, a London King's Cross–Leeds train was coming the other way, also at speed; although warned by detonators and red lights of the first accident, it could not stop in time, and so ran through the debris. In the double collision 14 passengers were killed, mostly when the third train hit the pile of wreckage.

The primary cause was snow; although the signalbox levers were standing in the 'danger' position, the snow blocked the slots on the signal posts so that the signal arms were jammed at 'clear'. The Abbots Ripton disaster brought about a great change in UK train signalling: thereafter the procedure became that the signalbox ahead was asked whether the line was clear before a train was sent forward, rather than relying on the assumption that the line was clear unless a train was known to be in the section ahead.

At Castlecary, on the Edinburgh–Glasgow main line, the indication shown by a distant warning signal should have repeated the indications of the stop signals ahead. This information was questioned by two drivers. One train from Dundee had passed Castlecary stop signals at 'danger' although, as it had approached,

the signalman had held a red light towards the driver. The signalman assumed the train had not stopped, and so he accepted a following train, from Edinburgh, but making sure his signals were at 'danger'. This latter was a heavy express, hauled by one of the huge Flying Scotsman-type Pacific engines. To his horror it, too, did not stop at his first signal. Unknown to him, the Dundee train had in fact stopped at the far end of the station. The Edinburgh train hit the back of the Dundee train and overrode several of its coaches; moreover, some of the leading coaches of the Edinburgh train passed over the top of its engine. Casualties were heavy: 35 died and 179 were injured.

Somehow, the engine crew of the Edinburgh train survived, being protected by the big cab and tender of their express engine. The engine crews of both locomotives were absolutely adamant that the distant signal had shown 'clear', meaning to them that the stop signals ahead likewise indicated 'clear'. Quite what had been shown by the distant signal was never established – although it worked normally afterwards. Did the snow play a part, perhaps building up on the wire so that the signal arm went to 'clear'. Or maybe the snow on the lamp glass made the yellow signal seem green? Whatever the case, the subsequent inquiry recommended the adoption of Welwyn control (see page 40) to help prevent signalmen's errors as well as the automatic warning system (AWS), which would help drivers at distant signals.

Left: Two trains ran past the signals at 'danger'; one stopped, and the other collided with it at Castlecary in 1937. Coaches of the second train overrode the locomotive and finished up on top killing 35 people. Snow interfering with the working and sighting of signals was suggested as a cause.

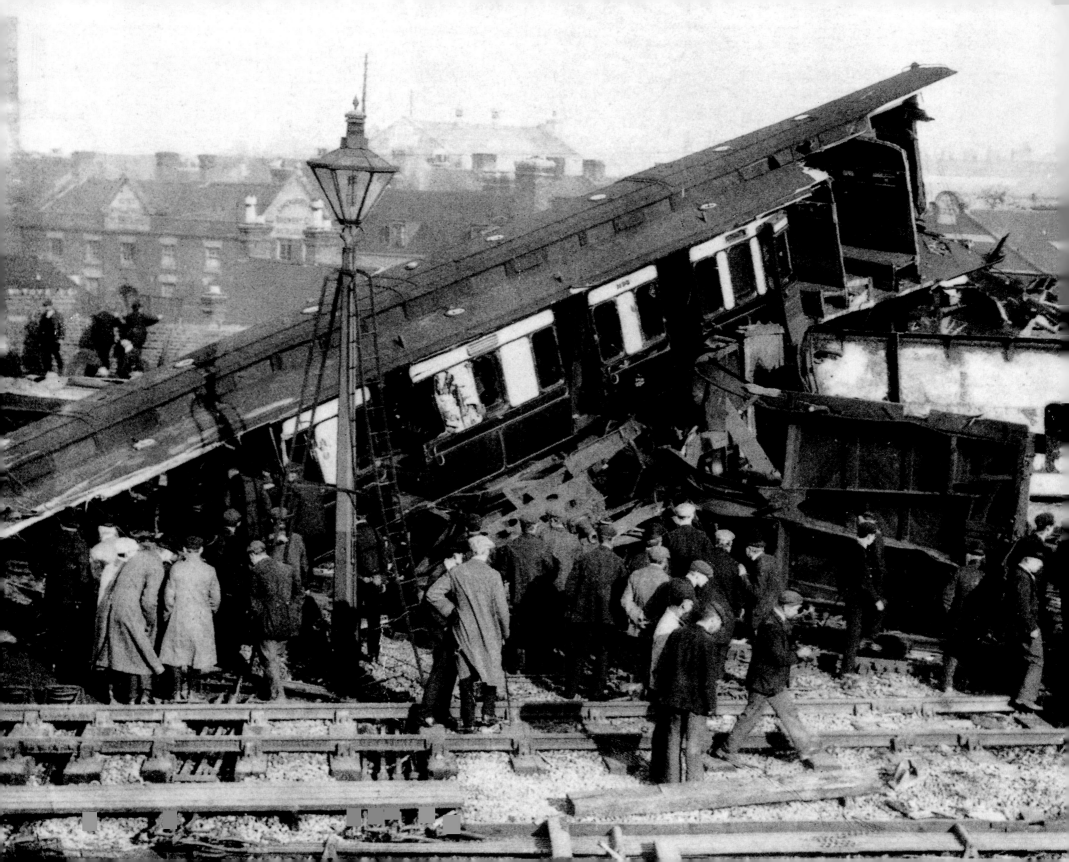

CHAPTER 9

GREAT MYSTERIES

In the UK, by autumn 1907, there was great concern when the newspapers reported yet another high-speed wreck of a passenger train, the third in 16 months. What was going wrong? Even today we have no real idea why these tragedies happened. Drivers undoubtedly made mistakes in these and other accidents discussed in this chapter, but they and their firemen (if there was a second person with the driver) were killed and so we do not know what those mistakes were. Other witnesses could fill in some details, such as the speed at which the train was travelling when it crashed – it should have been moving much slower than it was, or should perhaps have stopped altogether – but still, we will never find out precisely what was going on in the driver's cab. We know whether or not the brakes were applied, but not why they were not applied in time to bring the train down to the correct speed. Was the driver or fireman taken ill? Was there some other emergency which distracted them? Were they simply not paying attention to the signals or their location?

Three British wrecks: Salisbury, Grantham, and Shrewsbury

At Salisbury on 1 July 1906 a boat-train containing passengers off an Atlantic liner was running from Plymouth to London Waterloo. At the time there was fierce competition for this particular traffic between the Great Western Railway (GWR) and the London & South Western Railway (LSWR). The GWR planned to open its new shorter route to Plymouth a day later. Did the LSWR set out to show the GWR that it could run the boat-trains just as quickly? There is no way to know.

At the London end of Salisbury Station the line from Plymouth curved sharply to the left, and there was a permanent 30 mph (50 kmh) speed restriction. Whether the boat-train driver forgot it or did not realize how fast he was travelling (UK steam engines did not normally have speedometers) is a mystery. Whatever the truth, this particular boat-train approached Salisbury at over 60 mph (100 kmh). The driver and fireman had not fallen asleep – of that there was no doubt, for the engine

Left: The high speed derailment at Shrewsbury in 1907 resulted in a mountain of wreckage as coaches piled up one on top of another.

Right: At Salisbury in July 1906 a Plymouth–London boat train overturned on the sharp curve and the wooden coaches simply fell apart, killing over half of the 43 passengers on board.

Above: The unexplained failure of a train to stop at Grantham in 1906 led to it being diverted through sharply curved points on to a branch line where it derailed. Part of the train fell down an embankment and most of it caught fire.

Instead of slowing down, the Edinburgh express roared through the station. A signalman saw both the driver and the fireman standing in their normal places on the engine. The points were still set towards Nottingham as the train shot past the 'danger' signals and over the sharply curved crossover. The tender of the engine derailed, the leading three coaches piled up against the engine, and following coaches were catapulted down an embankment. Both groups of coaches caught fire because of burning coal and escaping gas. 12 people plus the engine crew died.

At Shrewsbury the main line from Crewe comes into the station from the north on a tight left-hand curve; there were points there as well as even sharper curves to the extreme left-hand platform tracks. A 10 mph (16 kmh) speed restriction was imposed. Nevertheless, in the early hours of 15 October 1907 the 01.20 from Crewe not only failed to stop at 'danger' signals showing at the signalbox approaching Shrewsbury – the junction signalbox at the convergence of the Crewe and Chester lines did not have a 'clear' line – but also ran past them at high speed. The train overturned on the sharp curve, throwing coaches across several tracks. The engine crew were killed, as were 16 other people on the train, including mail-sorting staff in the postal vans.

Three US mysteries

One of the worst US single-line disasters, at Nashville on 9 July 1918, is a great mystery since, yet again, none of the enginemen survived. Standing instructions insisted that local passenger trains had to keep out of the way of expresses. On a long passing loop at Nashville a local train was scheduled to cross an express train coming in the opposite direction; if the express was late the local had to wait until it appeared. Why, on this day, the local train did not wait, instead continuing onto the single line, is something that has never been resolved. The local and the express met head-on at a combined speed of about 100 mph (160 kmh). Inevitably casualties were high: over 100 people were killed, making this the worst accident in terms of casualties that the USA has ever experienced.

The derailment of a New York Central (NYC) express from New York to Chicago on a sharp curve in April 1940 had echoes of the UK high-speed wrecks at Salisbury and Shrewsbury some 30 years earlier. This NYC line was known as the Water Level route since it followed river valleys as it headed north to Albany and then west alongside the Mohawk River where it cut through the Appalachian mountains towards Rochester. The four-track

whistle screamed through the night air as the train sped to disaster through the station, rolling to the right on the sharp left-hand curve and overturning, killing over half the 43 passengers as well as the engine crew.

Just over two months later, on 19 September, a London King's Cross–Edinburgh sleeping-car and mail train was booked to stop at Grantham at 23.00. Just north of Grantham Station were points designed to take the Nottingham line off the main East Coast line to the north. As a goods train from the Nottingham direction was signalled onto the southbound main line the interlocking required the facing points on the opposite down or northbound main line also to be set towards Nottingham, but the signals at the north end of the platform were set at 'danger' against the express from King's Cross with the warning distant signals further back showing 'danger, stop at next signal'. The express driver should not have been surprised to find signals instructing him to stop ahead, since he should have stopped at the platform anyway. By the time his mail and passengers had been loaded, the line would have been clear towards the north.

main line kept closely to the river; where the river turned at Little Falls the railway curved sharply, and there was a 45 mph (72 kmh) speed restriction. Despite warning signals marking this restriction – not to mention cab warnings that were acknowledged by the driver – he seemed oblivious of the need to slow down. The locomotive and 11 of the train's 14 coaches were scattered across the four tracks, with several being severely damaged. The 30 people killed included the driver and there were many serious injuries.

Open bridge spans caused several early disasters, as we have noted. By 1958 signalling was much improved, with automatic warning systems (AWSs), and in some places there was automatic train control, which in certain conditions (although these safety add-ons were not universal) actually imposed speed limits on a train. At lifting bridges special trap switches were set to derail a train if it overran 'danger' signals, thus stopping it (in theory) before it reached the open part of the bridge.

But no precaution is foolproof. On the morning of 15 September 1958, at Newark Bay, New Jersey, the driver of a diesel-hauled commuter train heading for New York failed to heed the warning of a distant signal, continued past a stop signal that was at 'danger', and then ran through the derailer switches at such a speed that his two locomotives and two of the five coaches went into the water at an open lift bridge. Including four train crew, 48 people died. How could the driver have failed to act in response to two signals and not seen an open lift bridge?

RECOMMENDATIONS

More extensive use of AWS/ cab signalling, better training of drivers and better discipline were the three factors which might have prevented the Nashville, Little Falls and Newark Bay accidents.

Left: Rescue came too late for 48 passengers on this commuter train which plunged into the river at Newark Bay in the USA in September 1958. The driver failed to stop at a danger signal warning of the open lift bridge.

Above: Heavy lifting gear gently hauls away wreckage so that rescuers can get further into the pile of mangled coaches to check for more survivors after the three-train collision at Harrow in October 1952.

The Harrow disaster, UK, 1952

The double collision on 8 October 1952 at **Harrow & Wealdstone Station, 11 miles (18 km) north-west of London Euston** on the West Coast main line to Scotland, was, at the time, Britain's worst peacetime railway disaster. Yet, just as at Newark six years later, the engine crew causing the disaster failed to act on a colour-light distant-warning signal which indicated 'caution' and that the driver should be prepared to stop at the next signal if it showed 'danger'. It was a misty morning and the rising sun must have been brightly in the driver's face as the overnight sleeping-car train from Perth to

London approached Harrow. That said, we simply do not know whether anything happened to distract the locomotive crew or whether the driver failed to see the distant signal's light against the bright misty background. The next signal, a mile (1.6 km) or so ahead, was at 'danger': a local steam train had crossed from the slow line to the fast line ahead of the Perth train to make its regular stop in the platform at Harrow.

The Perth express suddenly emerged out of the mist at about 60 mph (100 kmh) just as a host of commuters were boarding the local train, which was already well filled. The engine ploughed through the local's back three coaches and partly overturned. Within a minute or so another express, this one from Euston to Liverpool and Manchester and hauled by two engines – also travelling at about 60 mph (100 kmh) and with no chance of stopping – came the other way, and hit the shambles. The two engines reared up as they smashed into the already damaged engine of the Perth train, carried away a span of the footbridge above the tracks, and turned on their sides across the adjacent platform and onto the tracks of the local electric line. . . where a fourth train was luckily stopped before it too became involved.

There was now a massive pile of wreckage: the remains of 13 coaches were compressed into a space about 130 ft (40 m) long, 50 ft (15 m) wide and 30 ft (9 m) high, with the Perth engine underneath. Including three of the enginemen, among them the crew of the Perth train, 112 people were killed and about 150 were injured, many of them seriously. Because many railway employees used the local train to get to work, some railway offices at Euston headquarters lost their entire staff. Of those who survived, numerous people owed their lives to the rescuers, who included a US Army team that happened to be based nearby. We know what happened at Harrow, but the 'why' will remain forever a mystery.

This accident hastened the adoption of the automatic warning system (AWS) on British Railways.

The greatest mystery of all: Moorgate, 1975

From the opening of London Underground soon after the turn of the century, automatic devices were provided to stop trains if they went past signals at 'danger'. But the need to provide an automatic stop for anything more than a low-speed misjudgment at a dead-end station was something never even thought about. Why should it be? Drivers bring their trains to a safe stop at terminal stations thousands of times a day on the London Underground: it's a matter of routine. That was until 08.46am on 28 February 1975.

A train on the short Moorgate branch from Drayton Park, where trains shuttled back and forth over a line 2¾ miles (4.4 km) long, approached the platform but, instead of slowing down, accelerated and ran into the short overrun tunnel beyond the platform to hit the end wall of the tunnel with such force that the front three coaches were compressed into a compact mass of twisted metal. Matters were made worse because the tunnels had originally been built for full-size main-line trains; the smaller coaches of the tube train jack-knifed into the tunnel roof.

Rescue conditions were dreadful because of the confined space. With so many passengers trapped within the mess, cutting equipment was difficult to use. It took over 13 hours to get to all the survivors, and a full four days to reach the body of the driver.

This has been London Transport's worst accident: 42 passengers and the driver were killed, and 74 other people were injured. We know what happened: the driver applied power instead of the brakes as the train ran through the platform. But this was not a mistake, as at the disaster at Wadenswil (see page 56), for on London Underground the power and brake handles were separate. Before the crash the driver was seen standing at the controls and looking straight ahead. There was even speculation that he had decided to commit suicide, but the inquest jury returned a verdict of accidental death.

If he intended suicide, why? And why should he wish to take so many others with him? We shall never know.

Above: The disaster at Moorgate on the London Underground in February 1975 was one of the most traumatic faced by the rescue services since the Second World War. It took over 12 hours to get to the last of the survivors, who were trapped in the tightly packed wreckage, and further three and a half days to release the driver's body.

CHAPTER 10

CHRISTMAS TRAGEDIES

Christmas is a time when families get together for the festivities. This means that many people are travelling, whether going to stay with relatives or simply to have a few days' holiday. Today all this means extra traffic by road, air, ferry and, to a lesser extent now, train. Whatever form of transport is involved, Christmas brings its own unique problems, since the extra travellers all want to move together in a peak period culminating on Christmas Eve and returning soon after Christmas Day.

All this throws considerable strains on public transport, and in the past the rail networks bore the brunt of this. Regular trains at Christmas were often run in two or more parts, or additional services were arranged; the latter might run through to distant branch lines normally served only by a local shuttle train that connected with a main-line service. The Christmas frenzy meant more trains had to be run and imposed immense strains on staff and resources. Often no automated aids were available, and so it was vital that signalmen and train crews were extra vigilant.

One of the earliest Christmas disasters on the railways occurred in 1841 at Sonning on the Great Western Railway main line from London Paddington to Bristol. On 24 December 1841 a train ran into an earth-slip in the great cutting just on the London side of Reading. The train, really supposed to be just for goods traffic, had left Paddington at 04.30. It included, however, two third-class carriages next to the tender. In reality these were little more than wagons whose sides were only 2ft (60 cm) above the floor and whose bench seats were quite open to the weather and

> The Strasbourg express was headed by one of the largest locomotives in France, a huge 4-8-2. Most of the coaches of the Nancy train were destroyed as this leviathan rode over them. The collision at Lagny was France's worst peacetime rail disaster: no fewer than 230 passengers died and 300 were injured.

Left: Fire was always the enemy when gaslit coaches were involved in accidents. Twisted metal and a pile of ash was all that was left of some of the coaches involved in the Hawes Junction collision high on the Pennines on Christmas Eve 1910.

cinders from the engine. Eight passengers were killed when the goods wagons impacting from behind crushed the coaches.

The Hawes Junction collision, 1910

Back in 1910 the Midland Railway main line from London St. Pancras via Leeds and Carlisle going on to Edinburgh and Glasgow provided a third route to Scotland through the centre of the UK; it was a rival to the East Coast route from King's Cross and the West Coast route from Euston. Between Leeds and Carlisle the line had to climb up and through the Pennines, reaching a summit of about 1100 ft (330 m) above sea-level at Ais Gill. From the south there was a fairly steady climb on relatively easy gradients from Leeds, but from Settle there were 15 miles (25 km) of stiff climbing at an almost unbroken 1 in 100. There followed 10 miles (16 km) of slight ups and downs along the top of the Pennines through what was then known as Hawes Junction (more recently renamed Garsdale) to Ais Gill; thereafter there was an abrupt descent at 1 in 100 for 15 miles (25 km) down the other side to Appleby.

This steep climb over the Pennines was one of the causes of the Hawes Junction disaster in the early hours of Christmas Eve 1910. The Midland Railway had only small engines and often required two of them to haul the heavier trains up the

steep gradients. Hawes Junction, in the top section, was the place where the assisting engines taken off the trains at Ais Gill were turned so that they could be sent back to their base stations at Carlisle or Leeds.

That morning nine engines were in Hawes Junction engine yard, waiting to be sent back, including two which had arrived from Ais Gill; these had been taken off trains from Carlisle and had been turned and coupled together ready to go back there. Traffic was heavy: there were extra Christmas passenger trains on top of the regular passenger and goods trains. The signalman managed to get the two engines out of the yard and beside the branch-line platform. After goods trains in each direction on the main line and an extra passenger train heading for Scotland had passed there were a spare few minutes to signal the two engines out onto the northbound track. But, until the extra passenger train had cleared the three-mile (5 km) block section to Ais Gill, the two engines could not be sent away – they had to be held at Hawes Junction's down advanced starting signal.

Hawes Junction was a bleak, exposed place at the best of times. That night, with heavy rain and a howling wind, it was awful. There were other trains on the southbound line and more engines to get away back to Leeds, and in the generally vile conditions the signalman forgot the two engines destined for Carlisle. He was offered a sleeping-car train from the south, and passed on the bell signals to Ais Gill, which accepted the train. He cleared the signals for the express, and naturally the drivers of the two engines took this as permission to start off. They didn't go all that fast – perhaps at 30 mph (50 kmh). The double-headed sleeping-car train, travelling at twice that speed, soon caught up, just after they had passed through a tunnel. Even if the leading express driver did see the red tail-lamp on the back engine ahead, he had little time to brake before he ran into it.

The leading engine of the express was derailed. The second engine went over on its side and the wooden-bodied coaches piled up behind it. Most of the coaches were gaslit, so the wreckage soon caught fire: 12 passengers were either killed on the spot or died later, and over 20 were injured.

The outcome of this accident was a call to eliminate gas lighting (a call that was still being made nearly 20 years later after another collision and fire on the Midland line to Bristol) and one of the first real recommendations for the installation of track circuits to help prevent signalmen from forgetting trains they could not easily see. At Hawes Junction, however, the crews of the two engines were also at fault: according to the famous Rule 55, one of the most important in the book before the widespread adoption of track circuits, they should have reminded the signalman that their engines were standing on the main line.

Collision at Lagny, France, 1933

Fog has always been the enemy of signalmen and drivers, especially before signalmen were assisted by track circuits or other devices to detect trains. For drivers, peering for signals in fog was difficult and nerve-racking, especially in the days when all that were available were dim oil lamps. It was really because of fog that the various forms of automatic train control and warning systems were originally developed. In the UK the Great Western Railway was one of the pioneers of this form of assistance for drivers. In France from the 1920s a form of AWS was in use: an electric current was passed through a contact on the locomotive that rubbed over an electrified ramp on the track at distant or 'warning' signals.

This makes the Lagny disaster all the more of a mystery. In 1933 Christmas was on a Monday, and many people were travelling to visit friends and relatives on the preceding Saturday evening, 23 December. That evening was cold, frosty and very foggy. Trains in and out of Paris Gare de l'Est were in chaos: some were running late and there were extras to be fitted in. One particular train, from Paris to Nancy, was already two hours late when it started. It had not travelled very far through the Paris suburbs before being further delayed when checked or stopped by various signals.

It was just getting away from a signal check near Lagny, 17 miles (27 km) out of Paris, when the following from Paris–Strasbourg express, running at about 60 mph (100 kmh), charged out of the fog and straight into the back of the slower train causing havoc.

The Strasbourg express was headed by one of the largest locomotives in France, a huge 4-8-2. Most of the coaches of the Nancy train were destroyed as this leviathan rode over them. The collision at Lagny was France's worst peacetime rail disaster: no fewer than 230 passengers died and 300 were injured.

The mystery is why the Strasbourg train had passed 'caution' signals and a 'danger' signal before colliding with the train ahead. Perhaps the AWS failed in the icy conditions. The driver of the Strasbourg train was charged with manslaughter, but found not guilty.

Opposite: Repair gangs clear up the wreckage near Hawes Junction after an overnight express ran into the back of two engines running more slowly ahead of it.

Opposite: Although the original British Railways Mark 1 coaches were of all-steel construction, they could not withstand the impact of a heavy diesel locomotive in the collision at Coppenhall Junction on Boxing Day 1962.

Collision at Genthin, Germany, 1939

The collision that occurred at Genthin, 40 miles (65 km) west of Berlin on the Berlin–Magdeburg main line, in the early hours of 22 December 1939 bore remarkable similarities to that at Lagny, six years earlier. Once again Christmas was on the Monday. Although this was the first winter of the Second World War, passenger traffic was busy, with civilians travelling home or to relatives and service personnel who were not on active duty taking the opportunity to enjoy a brief leave with their families. Trains were heavily loaded: while Christmas extra trains were not laid on – military requirements took priority, of course – some of the ordinary trains had extra coaches.

As at Lagny, the night of Thursday 21 December was bitterly cold and with patchy fog. As Thursday became Friday, the 23.15 from Berlin Potsdam to Cologne was losing time because of signal checks and as it approached Genthin it was nearly 30 minutes late. The driver of the following express from Berlin to Kassell was making much better time, taking chances with some of the signals that cleared as he approached them. But he failed to see the warning signals at Belicke – the station before Genthin – and ran past a stop signal which was set at 'danger'. When he got to Genthin he saw 'clear' signals – still 'clear' for the train ahead, which was just approaching them. The staff at Genthin, having been warned that the second train had run past signals at 'danger', showed a red light towards it; unfortunately, this was seen by the crew of the first train, who stopped.

The second express appeared out of the fog and went straight into the front train at 60 mph (100 kmh). The big 4-6-2 locomotive threw the back coaches of the Cologne train into the air, and they landed on top of it in a pile of broken timber and bent metalwork. Coaches that were not destroyed were thrown around in front of and behind the 4-6-2. Casualties were heavy: 186 people were killed and 101 severely injured. This was Germany's worst railway disaster. The driver of the second train spent three years in prison for his lack of caution; this was not the first time he had passed signals at 'danger'.

That was not the only major tragedy on German railways that day. In the south of the country, near Lake Constance, two trains met head-on at speed and 101 people died.

Collision at Coppenhall Junction, UK, 1962

Boxing Day 1962, and many passengers were returning from their Christmas break – those were the days when normal work resumed on 27 December. On the West Coast main line, north of Crewe, southbound trains were bunching up because of frozen points around Crewe Station. Signalling had by this time been modernized with full track circuiting, a number of signals worked automatically and, although some of the old signalboxes controlled the new signals by levers, there was none of the offering-and-acceptance procedure the old block system had used. Each signal acted in conjunction with the one ahead. If a first signal was at red, the signal behind it showed a single yellow as a warning, and the one behind that showed a double yellow as a preliminary warning. All signals had AWS magnets on the track.

An electrically hauled Liverpool–Birmingham train had been stopped at several signals. Even though the line was track-circuited, the crew had to call the signalman by telephone at the signal if they were delayed. The driver duly did so and was told to wait for the signal to go to 'clear'. After a while it did, and the train moved forward to the next signal. The following Glasgow–London diesel-hauled train was soon at a stand at the signal behind the Birmingham train. Unfortunately, however, the telephones were by then not working: a receiver had not been put back properly. Instead of trying the telephones at the signals on an adjacent line, the driver of the London train decided to go forward under stop-and-proceed rules.

By then it was dark and bitterly cold. The London train went forward. The driver could see the next signal ahead was at red, but, when he was part of the way towards it, it changed to single yellow. What he did not see until the last minute was the Birmingham train, which had been standing waiting for the signal to change. Although the driver of the London train thought he was travelling at no more than 6 mph (10 kmh) he hit the Birmingham train with such force that its back two (all-steel) coaches telescoped, killing 18 passengers and seriously injuring 34.

The driver of the London train was held responsible for the disaster: he had not ensured the line was clear; he had not thought to use alternative telephones; and, it was concluded, he had travelled too fast once he had decided to go forward.

CHAPTER 11

ACCIDENTS WITHOUT FATALITIES

Most of the accidents so far discussed occurred because someone was not concentrating on what they were doing, or assumed something had happened when in fact it had not. A few disasters have been the result of equipment failures, but more developed from accidents into tragedies because of the equipment and materials used at the time: often, as we have frequently noted, disasters have led to improvements in this area, as, for example, the replacement of cast-iron by wrought-iron and then by steel. Wooden frames and bodies made railway carriages a death trap if there was an accident: timber was often broken into small pieces and offered passengers no protection if the carriage was hit by the engine of another train, while oil and gas lighting could all too easily set wooden-bodied coaches ablaze.

Left: Accidents often happen through carelessness: these Class 31 diesel locomotives were left unattended without their brakes applied properly. They rolled along a siding, through bufferstops and down on to the M1 motorway in London in October 1988, without injuries.

Although there was severe damage underneath as the bogies were ripped off, only a few panes of glass in the windows were broken. There was some crushing to the coach ends, but the basic shells remained intact. Although 48 passengers were injured, not a single person was killed.

In the years since the Second World War safety considerations have been applied far more stringently. All-metal bodies for coaches – sometimes steel, sometimes aluminium – have replaced wood, and the latest designs in the UK and in some other countries are of integral construction; i.e. they are self-supporting and so form a box structure of immense strength which will not break up if there is an accident. Automation of signalling procedures and equipment now provides not merely the ability to prevent errors by signalmen in normal working, but can also allow total control of a railway, with computers – fed by data concerning train location, speed, direction, etc. – triggering the commands to set points and clear signals.

Many railways, however, do not have automation capable of eliminating all the consequences of driver error. Certainly such technology is available, but it is extremely expensive. Much discussion continues between railway managements and governments about whether the expense of adding full automation to an existing railway can be justified considering how few lives would be lost in one of the very rare collisions, especially since modern coaches enclose passengers in a very safe environment. In some years, in some countries, not a single passenger is killed in a train accident. Nevertheless, on many new lines – as in Japan, Germany and France and through the Channel Tunnel – signalling is so automated that it takes over from the driver to slow down or stop a train if he fails to act in time.

In the last two decades there have been some spectacular high-speed accidents which have resulted in no fatalities at all.

In February 1980 the electrically hauled 20.25 train from London Euston to Manchester, running down the West Coast main line, was only 15 minutes out from Euston. As it approached Bushey it was travelling at just under 100 mph (160 kmh). A welded rail-joint had fractured and a gap had opened up between the rails – enough of a gap that, as the locomotive wheels clattered over it, the rail bent and the entire nine-coach train was derailed. Carriages were thrown in all directions. The middle ones separated and turned onto their

Above: The overturned coaches after the 100 mph (160 kmh) derailment at Bushey in north-west London in 1980. The coach bodies remained structurally intact, only a few windows were broken, there was no fire and nobody was killed – an astonishing tribute to the strength of modern British coaches.

sides. Luckily the coaches (other than the restaurant car, which just as luckily stayed upright) were of Mark 2 and Mark 3 designs, dating respectively from the late 1960s and the 1970s, and thus had all-steel integral bodies. Although there was severe damage underneath as bogies were ripped off, only a few panes of glass in the double-glazed windows were broken, so that no passengers were thrown out. There was some crushing and damage to the coach ends, but the basic shells remained intact. Although 48 passengers were injured, not a single person was killed. What a contrast to the consequences of the broken rail at Hither Green in 1967 (see page 68).

Even more remarkable was the collision at Colwich, also on the West Coast main line but much further north, between Lichfield and Stafford. In September 1986 a London Euston–Manchester train overran a signal at 'danger' and

stopped with the front of its electric locomotive just on a diamond crossing as it turned off the main line to the right. This meant that the engine was fully in the path of the southbound main line from Crewe, on which there was a Liverpool–London train approaching at 100 mph (160 kmh). The locomotive of the Liverpool train, also an electric, hit the standing engine head-on. The Liverpool locomotive was thrown to the left of the line and seven coaches out of the 12 behind it went over the top of the leading coaches of the Manchester train. Two of the Liverpool coaches were catapulted as far as the fifth coach of the Manchester train; the others formed a mound of wreckage which also included the front two coaches of the Manchester train. This was one of the most destructive accidents for many years in terms of written-off rolling stock. But not a single passenger was killed.

RECOMMENDATIONS

Despite the remarkable performance of the Mk 2 and Mk 3 coaches, the inquiry still required improvements, most notably in various aspects of maintenance, especially track welds.

Left: Although the coach bodies remained intact, the undergear and bogies were badly damaged in the Bushey derailment. It was fortunate that no other train was approaching since other tracks were blocked by the derailed train.

18 November 1996 outside influences showed how vulnerable the tunnel was to fire.

A lorry on board a shuttle train designated for freight traffic, was seen to have a small fire as the train left the French terminal near Calais and entered the tunnel bound for the Folkestone terminal in England. It took about 10 minutes for the control centre to be advised of the fire and for the train driver to be contacted by radio and told of the fire. By that time the shuttle train was about a third of the way down the tunnel and the fire was well alight. Initial safety rules said that the driver should continue to try and get out of the tunnel at the far end for the fire to be dealt with in the open. But a warning was given on the locomotive that the stabilising jacks on one of the wagons used during loading and unloading were starting to lower (a false alarm as it turned out, caused by the fire). The driver had to stop, as near as he could to one of the cross passages. The second line of defence would have been to uncouple behind the passenger coach in which the lorry drivers were travelling, next to the locomotive, and to go forward leaving the wagons behind, but traction power was lost when the overhead conductor wires were short circuited so that the train could not move.

The fire had become an inferno near the back of the train with several lorries burning fiercely and an immense amount of smoke. But the passenger coach was sealed and smoke only entered when the train captain opened a door to see what was happening. Air in the tunnel is controlled by huge fans and when the air flow was reversed they drew the fumes away from the passenger coach and allowed the train crew and 30 or so lorry drivers to evacuate the passenger coach to the safety of the service tunnel. The air in the service tunnel is kept at a higher pressure than the rail tunnels to stop fumes from a fire from entering. Just 20 minutes after the train stopped everybody was in the service tunnel, some suffering from smoke inhalation when the door of the passenger coach was opened. But nobody died. What a contrast to the 1987 King's Cross station fire (see page 73). Sure, there are lessons which must be learned from the Channel Tunnel fire, but the safety procedures worked.

The circumstances of the accidents in this chapter can be related to others of years past with old style wooden coaches and the fire hazard which caused so many deaths and injuries. Today's new trains are generally stronger and fire resistant, and with better track, more automation and more assistance to prevent driver's mistakes, railways can truly claim to be the safest form of transport.

Above: One of the fire-damaged locomotives of the lorry shuttle train which caught fire in the Channel Tunnel in November 1996.

Opposite: The blaze was so fierce that it engulfed several wagons and their lorries and badly damaged a length of one of the rail tunnels. However, the safety procedures worked and the lorry drivers in the passenger coach were able to get to the service tunnel for rescue.

Just a few accidents have occurred in France on the TGV (Trains à Grand Vitesse), which can travel at up to 186 mph (300 kmh): a level-crossing collision on an ordinary line on 23 September 1988 and two derailments on high-speed lines, but without any spreadeagling of the coaches, which kept in line. In Germany one of the new Inter-City Express (ICE) high-speed trains was derailed in March 1993 across a junction, though at the time it was travelling at low speed. In all these instances there were no passenger fatalities and, except in the French level-crossing accident, no injuries.

The Channel Tunnel Fire, 1996

The 31 mile (50 km) Channel Tunnel linking the railway systems of Britain and France consists of three tunnels, two single track rail tunnels on either side of a service and rescue tunnel in the centre. The service tunnel is linked to the continuous platforms in the rail tunnels every ¼ mile (350 metres) by cross passages, effectively making two 31 mile long stations. Everything possible was done to make the trains and the tunnels fire-proof. But on

Index compiled by Ian D. Crane